for Jim

Café de l'Aube à Paris

Dawn Café in Paris

Willis

PRAISE FOR WILLIS BARNSTONE

The Restored New Testament

"The always amazing Barnstone has outdone even himself in this beautiful, scholarly, yet profoundly subversive book."—Frederick Crews

"This heroic enterprise, an expansive single-handed edition of the New Testament, is a substantial addition to the sixty-odd publications of the poet and translator Willis Barnstone. It appears in company with the fourth edition of a collection called *Ancient Greek Lyrics*, which contains practically all of Sappho and a large selection of other lyric poets—"our earliest songs in European antiquity"—that Barnstone "helped into English nearly half a century ago. Barnstone also translates from Chinese, German, and Spanish. He has collaborated on editions of several Gnostic texts, including the Gospel of Thomas, of which the original survives in Coptic; and has worked on the Dead Sea Scrolls, on the Christian Apocrypha—books found in the Greek version of the Jewish Bible the Septuagint but excluded from the Hebrew canon."—Frank Kermode, *New York Review of Books*

"Barnstone's new English version of the core texts of Christian Scripture is almost startling in its freshness. He gives us a set of Gospel narratives that are bold and direct in their simplicity and that show how steeped the first Christians were in the Jewish world from which they derived."—Robert Alter

"In an achievement remarkable by almost any standard, and surely one of the events of the year in publishing, renowned poet and scholar Barnstone has created a new and lavish translation—almost transformation—of the canonical and noncanonical books associated with the New Testament....The high bar Barnstone has set for himself is the creation of an English-language Scripture that will move poets much as the 1611 King James Version moved Milton and Blake. Only time will tell if Barnstone has achieved his goal, but his work is fascinating, invigorating, and often beautiful. Essential."—*Library Journal*

"Willis Barnstone's *Restored New Testament* is breathtaking, new, astounding. It is a courageous, daring book."—Gerald Stern

The Gnostic Bible

"Willis Barnstone and Marvin Meyer's *Gnostic Bible* joins Bentley Layton's *Gnostic Scriptures* as one of the true critical sourcebooks for gnostic texts. Here, from China to Catalonia, from the first to the fourteenth centuries, gnosticism is seen as a global meditation."—Harold Bloom

"An enormously rich collection of sources—a wonderful achievement!" —Elaine Pagels

"Willis Barnstone has a problem: he's too good. Everything he writes, from his invaluable *The Other Bible*, a compendium of holy texts no writer should be without, through his brilliant translations and beautiful poems, is a breathtaking achievement."—Carolyn Kizer

Sweetbitter Love: The Poems of Sappho

"What a joy to have Willis Barnstone's *Sweetbitter Love*. This is not only a vivid, sensuously elegant translation of every scrap of Sappho we have; the wonderful introduction is designed to increase our ardor as well as our knowledge, and the appendix containing everything the ancients said of her as well as poetic tributes up through Baudelaire's is itself a treasure." —Alicia Ostriker

"Sappho knew what we never tire of learning: passion makes the moment eternal. Willis Barnstone has plumbed profound layers of the ancient Greek to bring us Sappho. On his way to her, he renewed the Gnostic Gospels and the Gospels proper. Now he has sounded the deepest lyric rock of our founding and given us new sound."—Andrei Codrescu

"Willis Barnstone has brought a life dedicated to translation and a lifetime of immersion in the Greek language to give us these new and inspired translations of Sappho. With its brilliant introduction and dazzling notes, this is the book of Sappho you will want on your bedside table."—David St. John

"I have this Sappho with me all the time now, as this collection is absolutely stunning in every respect, and I'm filled with gratitude to you for having borne it into the world. May your *Sappho* be blessed. It is a tremendous gift to all of us."—Carolyn Forché

"What amazes me is how Sappho's lyrics, composed in the seventh century B.C.E., transcend their time and place to enchant us now. In lines that are at once passionate and precise, seemingly artless and yet magical, she writes of the cycles of life and death, and of erotic desire as a sacred calling. She looks into the burning center of things, and expresses pure wonder in the evening star, the moon, birdsong. Willis Barnstone's masterful translations capture her excited praise for things of this world, making one of her prophetic observations shine with lasting truth: 'Someone, I tell you, in another time, / will remember us.'"—Grace Schulman

Algebra of Night: New and Selected Poems 1948-1998

"*Algebra of Night*! I just love this book. It is a dazzling cross section of his passionate wisdom and wit. With Borgesean scope and cunning, in free verse or invisible sonnets, Barnstone floats us to resonant surprise. Out of an extraordinary life and the richness of many languages, literatures and travels ranging over the world, this gorgeous energy of a poet of genius. I don't believe he sleeps!"—Ruth Stone

The Secret Reader: 501 Sonnets

"Four of the best things in America are Walt Whitman's *Leaves*, Herman Melville's *Whale*, the sonnets of Willis Barnstone's *Secret Reader*, and my daily Corn Flakes—the rough poetry of morning."—Jorge Luis Borges

"I think Willis Barnstone has been appointed a special angel to bring the "other" to our attention, to show how it is done. He illuminates the spirit for us and he clarifies the unclarifiable … I think he does it by beating his wings."—Gerald Stern

"If sonnets were windmills, give Willis Barnstone a knighthood and a horse with dreamy eyes, not for his victories alone, but because something in this book helps us get out of the snow and ice of our lives."—Stanley Moss

"A valuable accomplishment worthy of Borges who acts here as Barnstone's 'master.' These five histories build into a remarkable modernist testament."
—Edward Hirsch

"Through the lyricism and urgency of these 501 sonnets, something terribly human rises again and again, assuring us it is impossible to keep Willis Barnstone's *The Secret Reader* secret."—Yusef Komunuyakaa

"The stunning scope, their wonderful irreverence, their slangy, antic humor, their startling realism, and their brave confrontation with the ultimate questions all combine to bring us a worthy life work that is bound to be recognized as a masterpiece."—Philip Appleman

"Willis Barnstone is an American original whose recently completed volume of sonnets is a classic. A great achievement, reflecting a lifetime of commitment to the act of literature. It is filled with lyricism, passion, meditative wisdom, irreverence, blasphemy and unflinching compassion for the human condition. Clearly a tour de force"—D. M. Hertz

"His range of knowledge informs powerful social, religious and political commentary as he writes about philosophers and poets (especially but not solely Hispanic and Chinese), dead from AIDSs, Tibet, a Stone Age mummy found in a glacier and, of course, himself ("Do I hurt? NO, I'll be / a will-less barn stone cool and and on my own"). This prodigious effort offers rewards to grazers and those who read the sonnets in order."—*Publishers Weekly*

Modern European Poetry

"Willis Barnstone's *Modern European Poetry* brings together in one volume the best poetry composed in Europe in outstanding translation. I keep it as my favorite bedside volume."—W.S. Merwin

Café de l'Aube à Paris

Dawn Café in Paris

Poems Composed in French
+
Their Translation into English

WILLIS BARNSTONE

The Sheep Meadow Press
Rhinebeck, New York

Designed and typeset by The Sheep Meadow Press.
Distributed by The University Press of New England.

All inquiries and permission requests should be addressed
to the publisher:

The Sheep Meadow Press
PO Box 1345
Riverdale, NY 10471

Library of Congress Cataloging-in-Publication Data

Barnstone, Willis, 1927-
Cafe de l'aube a Paris - dawn cafe in Paris : poems / Willis Barnstone.
    p. cm.
ISBN 978-1-931357-90-6
I. Title.
PS3503.A6223C34 2011
811'.54--dc22

                          2011001396

Acknowledgments

At the end of WW2 my brother Howard Barnstone was a naval officer in Marseilles. He stayed a few years longer and was close to the photographer Henri Cartier-Bresson. Fifteen years later, by then an architect, Howard invited Bresson to Texas to do a book with him on the remarkable port city of Galveston, Texas. Soon appeared *The Galveston That Was* by Howard Barnstone, photographs by Henri Cartier-Bresson and Ezra Stoller, foreword by John James Sweeney (New York: Macmillan, 1965). Now the pendulum swings back to France—again through a book—whose cover photograph by Bresson reveals dawn and the Eiffel Tower seen from the balcony window of the photographer's Paris apartment.

I wish to thank those who generously read my manuscripts, caught errors and offered sage advice: Marc Hofstadter who was the first to see these poems; four marvelous French voices, Anne Celine Magnan-Park, Marianne Allain, Helène Cardona, and Laure Anne Bosselaar; my former colleagues in Romance Languages at Wesleyan University the late unequaled friend Carl Viggiani, and Norman Shapiro with whom I conspired in his version of Charles Baudelaire's *Les Fleurs du Mal*; and Antoine Cuvelier, photographer and scientist in Paris.

I also salute Florence Robert, editor at Éditions Denoël in Paris on the rue du Cherche-Midi where après-guerre I lived as a student. Over breakfast in a small bread-and-breakfast in Western Ireland, Florence Robert and Bruno read many of these poems and swelled my head.

pour Mort et Jeannette
sur la lune de la Seine

et les genoux d'Henri Peyre
où dormait mon enfant

❧

for Mort and Jeannette
on the moon of the Seine

and the knees of Henri Peyre
where my daughter slept

Table of Contents

La vie des poètes

Chambres des Orphelins

Life of the Poets

Rooms of the Orphans

Chant nocturne des Enfants Invisibles

Vignt cafés du monde et un à l'aube

AN AMERICAN IN PARIS

How can one explain how an American living between California and Indiana should, in a fit of four years, compose a book of poetry in French? The first step toward my lifelong foreign language binge began at an early age in Mexico when I became saturated with Spanish.

In the summer of 1943 my father and I drove down from Seattle, Washington, to a small silver-making Indian village, south of Tasco, deep in the mountainous heart of Mexico. We were led into a motel room by the owner, who closed the door behind us. Complete darkness. A sudden buzz and flutter of wings. *Bats!* dad shouted. We raced to the wall, fingered our way to a window, got the shutters open, two bats flew out into the moon. The mountains sighed. I yelled *¡patrón!* The owner blew in, flipped the switch and we had light. My Quaker boarding school Spanish had worked. The word *patrón* (boss) was the first word I remember saying in Spanish--or any foreign language--which at age fifteen I uttered with alarm. Then we reopened the window, just slightly.

Soon after this adventure, my father married a young Mexican, Marti Franco, which gave me a reason to return often to Mexico. Twice I worked for the American Friends Committee in Aztec villages, digging privies Then, in 1946 after my father's sudden death, I spent a year at the old Universidad Autónima in Mexico City, living in an orphanage for orphans of the Spanish Civil War. To support myself I taught English privately in the evenings, going to people's houses. The Spanish orphanage was locked up at ten. Many evenings I spent reading in all-night restaurants or I would camp on the floor of my stepmother's apartment in a poor barrio south of the Cathedral, sleeping on a tapete mat between the Indian maid and Marti's brother Sam, a captain in the Mexican army. Sam slept with his sunglasses on. Marti's mother, a Sephardim from Constantinople, spoke to me in Ladino, calling me *mancebico* (little lord), a word not heard in peninsular Spanish since the sixteenth century.

From fifteen on I was immersed in Spanish. That first language experience helped crucially, in grammar, phonetics, and confidence when in college I majored in French. Languages help each other, and learning one new tongue is a lesson for learning another. I was to add more to the endless pleasure of gathering words, living amid dictionaries and cultures, and knowing the ache of forgetting.

Spanish, French, Greek, Chinese, and German were addictions. I was exposed early. Absurdly many, of course, and I rarely was without a foreign dictionary in my pocket. I taught their literatures, translated the poets, and, through travel, book, and film, found excuses for keeping them up. French I began at age sixteen when I entered Bowdoin College in Maine. Later, I became guilty of huge absence from *la douce France*. That neglect and its partial redemption led to this book.

Because of World War II, we were all "accelerating," that is, jumping grades and taking extra courses to get more college in before being drafted. I was a freshman at sixteen in 1944. Just before my call-up date in '45, the war ended. I was free till the next war. To improve my French and add credits, I enrolled in the French School of the Middlebury College summer language program. I lived in its marvelous monolingual *Château* where the rule, there or anyplace on or off campus, was speak only French or expulsion. Somehow I bumbled toward graduation at Bowdoin and a diploma in Latin and was ready to wander into another continent. My mother staked me for the ship to Paris and an allowance for my year at the university. Ten dollars a week, a munificent sum in those days.

In September '48 I shared a four-man berth with goggling fish outside our porthole at the bottom of the *RMS Queen Elisabeth*, the largest passenger liner in the world. At our fun third-class level, where the dance and social action was, we were rocking our way over the angry north Atlantic to Le Havre. After six days I took the evening port train from Le Havre and reached Paris. The city was hit with a bus and metro strike and I decided to stay in the station hotel. Starving, at midnight I put on my Basque beret, went downstairs to the nearest bar, sat at the zinc (the bar), and saw hardboiled eggs racked above the croissants. I had ordered a late dinner of egg, bread, croissant, coffee, and cognac that the barman poured into the coffee. Everyone was out of film noir.

The hotel maid had flirted with me before I descended to my feast. The barman had the iron authority, tired eyes, and helpfulness that got me through my first mutterings in his language. I could not articulate it, but I intuited that in a hundred ways my destiny was Europe. As it turned out, I spent seven of the next ten years in Europe, most of the time speaking French.

LA RUE JACOB, 1948

La guerre était la bombe pour Apollinaire
qui envoyait ses lettres-poèmes des tranchées.
Un obus peigna ses cheveux dans un éclair
mais Guillaume à Paris se guérit enjoué
avec une cigarette aux lèvres comme une
ballade d'amour. Moi, j'espionnais la vie
de ma chambre de l'hôtel, un rouge tapis,
l'eau chaude dans le lavabo, au coin la lune
sur nous. Je soupirai ravi quand les chanteurs
des rues attrapaient la grêle des sous. La cour
puait fumée de pisse quand la pluie du soir
tomba des nuages bleus de vin. Nos draps trop courts
La grippe ravit le poète et nous le bonheur
comme Gui qui mourut le Jour de la Victoire.

LA RUE JACOB, 1948

War was fun for Guillaume Apollinaire,
sending letter poems from the trenches, yet
a bombshell came, gravely combing his hair,
but Guillaume healed in Paris, a cigarette
like a love ballad in his lips. I spied
life from a hotel room with a red rug,
hot water in the corner sink, and sighed
happy when the street singers used a jug
to catch the hailing francs. The courtyard reeked

with rising fumes of piss when evening rain
fell from the wine-blue clouds. Our sheets were far
too short. Fin de la guerre. Spanish flu creaked
into the poet's brain. We were young, zan-
y like Guillaume who croaked with La Victoire.

In Paris I first lived on rue Jacob, a cheap historic hangout, and became a graduate student in literature and philosophy at the Sorbonne, the University of Paris, in a plaza off Boul' Mich. To enroll I was told to go with my credentials to the concierge. In her small archival office, I waited to say *bonjour* to the formidable, spinally deformed lady. *Madame la concierge* was like any concierge checking one into the rundown hotels I would live in--quick, to the point, and no nonsense. *Votre diplôme, Monsieur.* Since my diploma was in Latin, she accepted it without translation, and stored it forever in the archives. I paid the eighteen dollars tuition fee, gave her a photo I'd taken at a *photomaton* in the métro. She stapled the picture to my student card, marked a small slip of paper with names of my professors, class titles and hour, handed me the schedule and my student card, and in three minutes I was back in the meeting place corridors of the thirteenth-century university.

In those corridors and in the plaza outside, I met my classroom friends. One afternoon a young Spanish student, whom I had talked to because I heard him speaking Spanish, was surprised that I knew the Spanish poets. At our second meeting he gave me his 1930s copy of *Espadas como labios* (Swords like Lips) by Vicente Aleixandre, the Spaniard's most accomplished early surrealist collection. This meeting, through book wisdom, was prescient. Over the years Aleixandre was my closest friend in Spain and the first person I'd see when in Madrid. I did a volume of his selected poems years before he was awarded the Nobel in poetry. Aleixandre was Spanish poetry during and after the disaster of the civil war.

When I stepped outside the Sorbonne main entranceway, a familiar sight was the din of young nuns in traditional robes, descending from their big French motorcycles, which they handled like toys. It gave French Catholics a fresh contemporary look. I recalled in a village outside Périgueux a nun leading nine- and ten-year-olds over a waving meadow, the kids singing in high squeaky gay chorus:

> Auprès de ma blonde
> Qu'il fait bon, fait bon, fait bon,
> Auprès de ma blonde
> Qu'il fait bon dormir.

> Lying by my blonde
> It feels good, feels good, feels good,
> Lying by my blonde
> It feel good to sleep.

I liked my red-carpeted rue Jacob room, but kept changing hotels, going from Jacob to rue Princesse to rue du Cherche Midi to rue de Vaugirard opposite the palaced Jardin du Luxembourg and to a hotel with the grand illogical name of l'Hôtel de Lisbonne et Portugal, all in the Quartier Latin on the Rive Gauche. Each place was within walking distance of the university and of the student, painter, poet, and novelist friends. Imagine promenading each school day along the rue de Prince where Paul Verlaine, "the prince of poets," lived and where he was found on his hotel room floor, dead drunk.

Morning was an awakening and foretold an event. In the evenings of soft autumn and blustery winter and amazing spring, Paris was inevitable surprise. We didn't party in our rooms, but went out on the town, talked, worked, were inebriated with learning and creating. Scott Fitzgerald and ee cummings were imitating our antics. We inhabited the enormous room of that intimate city of light and jazz. The vast Musée du Louvre, originally built in the seventeenth century as a theatre where Molière flourished for decades, became the Palais-Royal, the Palace of the Kings. It was a métro stop or brisk walk away. In the *toilettes* of the luxurious Louvre there was always up-to-date but fractured reading material, the toilet paper consisting of cut-up pages of recent issues of *Le Figaro* and *Le Monde*. The Mona Lisa, which one could look at in the

Louvre in solitude (she suffers now behind bulletproof glass and shouting crowds), revealed her silent powers, beholding us in her changing eyes. The Eiffel Tower, Paris's sun and moon, walked through the streets night and day, observing us from every angle,

> La tour Eiffel marche sur les rues
> de Paris dans la brume d'hiver.
> Ses lumières te font flotter nue
> au ciel de blé, courant dans l'air.
> La tour Eiffel marche sur les rues.

> The Eiffel Tower walks the streets
> of Paris in a winter fog
> and her light floats you to sky wheat
> and grass. Above the air you jog.
> The Eiffel Tower walks the streets.
>
> from "Shepherd of the Stars"

There was talk of the Romanian philosopher and pessimist thinker Emile Cioran. He was then only thirty-seven and had long ago repented and condemned his earlier *madness* as a Hitlerian admirer and Iron Guard Romanian nationalist. In Berlin he had been enthralled with Hitler and the 1934 putsch, "The Night of the Long Knives," when SS thugs executed hundreds and Hitler secured total power over Germany. A student at the University of Berlin, despite the prevailing anti-Semitism everywhere in Germany, he wrote his dissertation on a Jew, the French philosopher Henri Bergson[1]. When in 1937 he left

[1] Henri Bergson (1859-1941). Bergson was the most influential philosopher and teacher of his age. He was awarded the Nobel Prize in Literature (1927). His notions of intuition, élan vital and stream of consciousness were, according to his cousin Marcel Proust, the defining philosophical influence on his life. Bergson was in the air as we see in Virginia Wolfe and James Joyce who absorbed into their work his "stream of consciousness." In later life he developed a mystical notion of time, contrasting *durée*, time of the mind, with *temps*, mechanical time. He also drifted into Catholic theology. In 1940 he refused the Vichy offer to excuse him from anti-Semitic laws and he registered as a Jew and wore the Jewish star. When he died in 1941, he was buried, as he had ordered, in the Jewish cemetery in Paris. A Catholic priest said prayers over his grave.

In France I wrote my first collection of poems, published English lyrics in literary mags in Paris and London, and knew poetry would be my center. Six decades later, nothing has changed.

At the end of the school year, on the first day of June I married a Greek, Elli Tzalopoulou, in the mayor's office of the seizième arrondissement opposite St. Sulpice. In the fall we sailed to Greece for two years where the house language was French. Of course I also heard Greek, but both my mother- and father-in-law were fluent in French. Maria had gone to a French lycée in Constantinople and Basil had finished medical school in Paris. I taught French and English at the Anavryta Classical Lyceum outside of Athens where, among the thirty-two students, was nine-year-old Constantine, who was to become the weak brief-reigning king of Greece.

After Greece we were in Geneva where I worked for Les Editions Skira as a translator of art books from French into English. Then came a year in Andalusia in a medieval village south of Granada on the coast, and a stay in Prades in the French Catalonian Pyrenees during and after the Pablo Casals Festival. Then I disappeared into London as a full-time student at SOAS, the School of Oriental African Studies. After five years of roaming Europe, I came back to the States in 1953, just in time to hear Dylan Thomas read at the 92nd Street Poetry Center in Manhattan a few days before he died and the McCarthy hearings before Joe McCarthy faded away and died of acute alcoholism. I did and did not feel like the wanderer returned. New York was still my city, but not the only Ithaca of return. By now my roots were dispersed in many lands and tongues.

No sooner had I finished a graduate degree at Columbia when I was drafted for the Korean War. The Army sent me for the next years to France.

The first period was in Périgueux, just north of Le Midi, the South, meaning Provence. I took a small apartment in the ancient city with its Byzantine church. This was Montaigne country, a lyrical landscape yet authoritatively informed like a still life to be studied, like Montaigne himself, the master of the graceful essay. My mother and wife took a ship from New York to Athens. Elli said she looked radiant. Mother was to spend the year with us, which I looked forward to tremendously. She took sick on the ship. I got to Orly airport in Paris, where we met. Mother was returning immediately to the States. I hitched a ride on an American Army transport plane, easy to do in those days, and met her in the city. Ten days later, at Beth Israel Hospital, she was dead. We took a slow freighter back to France.

After a year our Air Force re-supply company was sent up north to a city in Normandy, Saint-André-de-l'Eure, not far from Paris, where I stayed till the end of my service. During these new French years, because I was the only French-speaking soldier on the base, the master-sergeant made me camp interpreter. I received our French hosts, talked to police to try to get GI's out of jams, and was sent all over town beginning with the mayor's office. I was not a spit-and-polish trooper, but I managed. The chance for constant rapport with the city was a wonderful turn. After twelve hours on duty, 6:00 AM roll call to the lowering of the flag and taps at 6:00, I was free. While basic training buddies were dodging death in Korea, I read novels by Colette, Mauriac and any good French book I could find. As in Périgueux I also worked to raise money on base and in town as I had in the south for local French social causes. One effective way was to have regular auctions on base for office equipment that was to be otherwise replaced. There were decent crowds, as much out of curiosity, that visited our unit, located off a small alley named for us, Boulevard Joseph Stalin. After the auction, the mother superior drove me out to their new children's hospital, a building with glass walls filled with sun overlooking a gentle landscape. I fell in love with the children, and it was almost unbearable to see in a great sunlit room the young beautiful girls lying in bed in a coma, faces still fresh despite interior devastation of their bodies, heads facing the ceiling, and dying of cancer.

I did not choose the good French assignment, but it was gold for a low-paid U.S. private first class, and I supplemented my income in the evenings by teaching an elementary course in French to enlisted men and officers for the University of Maryland Extension Program. I read the French poets in France, medieval to contemporary, all the fresh word or phrase. I was thinking, dreaming, writing in French, but always with dictionaries. Well, I am a dictionary nut in English too.

My journey to Paris and France began in 1948, only three years after WW2. The war was still on every wall and street and doorway. The air made it so. In speaking about these French poems infused with a postwar experience in ebullient Paris, I have not referred to the writers, artists, and composers who perished in concentration camps just a few years earlier. Most were Jewish but there were many besides the Jews who vanished in the death camps, like the surrealist poet Robert Desnos, who was arrested as active member of the French Résistance. Desnos was sent to four camps, Auschwitz, Buchenwald, Flossenburg, and finally to the showplace extermination center Terezín (Theresienstadt), near Prague. He was liberated but died two weeks later of typhoid, shortly before his forty-fifth birthday.

During the war years, Hollywood was reluctant to speak of the holocaust and extermination camps. The State Department was unwilling to release detailed information in their possession, but after Stephen Wise released details of the extermination camps, some knew what was happening. We were glued to papers, radio and the twice-a-week, seven- or eight-minute Paramount News before the feature movie. However, with school and adventures, the horrors were far off. But the moment I touched soil in France, there was no lack of reality. Many survivors in Central and Eastern Europe, especially in Germany and Poland, were still stranded in internment camps. Their homes had been seized or burnt and no one would take them into their country or village. These facts came out by then.

Some of my new writer friends were holocaust survivors. One was Bernard Citroën, the Dutch/French founder of a remarkable bilingual magazine *Points* that carried my first published poem in its founding issue. During the occupation Bernard hid for four years in a friend's basement. Even with flaming blond hair and false papers, he didn't dare step into the street. The poet Max Jacob (1876-1944), early key surrealist poet, was a close friend of Apollinaire and Modigliani, roomed for years with Picasso. He had converted to Catholicism back in 1909. When the Germans marched into Paris he hid in a monastery in the

Loire. Eventually he was betrayed by a local and picked up. He died at the internment camp at Drancy.

MAX JACOB THE DAY HE WAS SEIZED BY THE GESTAPO,
February 24, 1944,
at the St. Benoît-sur-Loire Monastery

Picasso painted all night long. You slept
and when the Spaniard took the bed at dawn
in the small furnished room you shared, you lept
back to the chair to scribble poems and yawn.
One bed and two young artists. You were poor
always. Then you saw light and moved your soul
in with the monks. You always played the fool
and wrote of butchers with binoculars,
dancing the streets of far Japan whose moon
had fleas. Your books shone in the libraries
of Paris—Max's caves. One afternoon
the Gestapo found you. Your monks tried to save
you. *J'ai ta peau!* you joked, mocking the lice
that bit you, bravely punning to the grave.

Isaak Babel similarly joked with his KGB captors when he was picked up at his dacha outside Moscow in 1939, or so the gallows humor tale has it, telling them at four in the morning, "What took you so long?" Many of those who did dare to step into the streets of Paris, like the brilliant, cheerful memoirist Helène Berr (1921-1945), author of *Journal*, did not make it. Berr was at the Sorbonne, finishing her doctorate on John Keats until her professor refused her entry to the class, but she stayed on in Paris, taking care of orphan children whose parents had been seized. She was picked up by the Gestapo as she left the métro station. She died in a camp. Here we have more than anecdote. We have the prophetic fears from her journal:

To think that if I am arrested this evening (which I've envisioned for a long time), I will be in Haute-Silésie in eight days, maybe dead, that my whole life will be suddenly extinguished with all the infinite I feel in me.

Hélène Berr Journal (1942-1944)

She died of typhus in Bergen-Belsen a few days before liberation, in the same camp where Anne Frank died of typhus a few weeks before her. After the Allies liberated Bergen-Belsen, they burnt it to rid the area of the disease. When I went back to France in the summer of 2008, I followed the tracks of Helène Berr, from street and métro to street and métro. Her book, which the French call the work of their Anne Frank, came out in 2007, sixty-five years after it was written[2]. The last poems added to the volume are about her,

> La Juive en sortant du métro
> avec son étoile mal cousue
> est saisie. Sombre Gestapo.
> Les mecs de menottes la saluent.

> The Jew coming up from the métro
> with her star too loosely sewn on
> is arrested. Black Gestapo
> whose handcuffs greet her with a frown.

from Jours de Paris, 1942

When I was possessed by the four-year fever of becoming, in my mind, a foreigner writing in French immediately after World War II, I tried to capture the France I knew first and best, the one recently liberated by Allied troops. The city of Paris in all its varied magnificence, from under-the-bridge clochards to students, artists and disdaining classes above them, almost did not survive. In August 1944 Adolf Hitler vowed to obliterate Paris as a few months earlier his army had systematically detonated Warsaw, the population fled and the city

[2] The international novel *Suite Française* by Irene Nemerovsky came out two years ago, about sixty-five years after she was captured in the forest but managed to give her suitcase and her two girls to a Christian nurse, who escaped and saved the children and the suitcase containing their clothes and the novel.

was debris. General Dietrich von Choltitz disobeyed Hitler, and he and his 17,000 German troops surrendered to French General Hauteclocke and Résistance leader Henri Roi-Tanguy.

Paris was saved, barely. Concerning that period, I'm old enough to remember when there was still postwar rationing of food and fuel in France and England, and in London every tenth lot on the average London block was a cleaned-up bomb site; when the currency in France floated adventurously in black market schemes from the *cité universitaire* to the *rue des Rosiers*; when the arts were as healthy as *pommes de terre*, and Molière and Lorca had no competition that could keep them out of the ordinary theatres. The ordinary person was more angry at the *flics* than polite to foreigners. I loved the rough manners, the workers' ruddy cheeks and iron hands, the noses of the habitual drinkers, the intellectuals' high nose and casual dress, the elegance of women of all ages and class, including grandmothers making it on sorry pensions. In the old wild days a strike or a march could be called for any time or on the hour. Jean Paul Sartre, an intellectual of many political flirtations, paraded once on Saint Germain Boulevard in sandwich boards that sang the virtues of Chairman Mao and the Great Proletarian Cultural Revolution. Albert Camus was essaying against the dangers of totalitarianism. Normal was debate in newspaper, book, the street, and jammed university halls of jeering and cheering students.

When the gangplank of the *Queen Elizabeth* opened in Le Havre and I wobbled down to a twilight pavement with a small suitcase, France gave passage to a foreigner. A month in Paris and "Willis" gave way to Guillaume. Being renamed was a treat, and for some lucky years I was an ordinary stranger in the street, not unlike the *étrangers* invented as the norm by the young Albert Camus. The quintessential French novelist was an *étranger* born to a Spanish mother in Algiers. When he was one, his French father was killed in the Battle of the Marne during the first World War. Spanish was his home language. He set his fiction in North Africa. Camus possessed a double vision of the world, even in his adopted Paris. His was Africa and Europe. And the world. In that cosmopolitan mix, an intimate circumference without border guards, I felt more than comfortable. A graduate student and *étranger* on the Rive Gauche, I was elated and free. My work in French and English was a mirror, like these later poems, of a double life. In Paris these poems had their source.

Willis Barnstone
Riverdale, New York
January 12, 2011

Dawn Café in Paris

I sleep and already live tomorrow. Must be
Monday. No, a beautiful negligent Sunday morning
and I dance with God, a beautiful woman

who tells me mouth to mouth in my soul
the banal secrets of my confusion,
and why I can't sleep, why forced to I get up

from sleep to speak to you in the black
in hours before the café of dawn who saves me
surely. I'm wrong. I kiss the mouth

of God. She is soft and doesn't blame me
that I die without hope. She assures me
that her presence isn't necessary, and I love her

devastated by her remoteness. I'm cold.
Remorseless winter lies on my knees.
I kiss a phantom. Warm, she is smiling.

Le train à Paris

Dans le train paquebot de nuit
du Havre à Paris, je suis assis
à côté d'une jeune femme de mon âge.
Elle est de Carpentras,
fille d'un sculpteur breton.
Nous avons la mort dans l'âme
après nos trois heures. Nous savons
que nous ne nous reverrons jamais plus,
mais elle se souviendra de moi,
de nos mains, et moi d'elle,
quoique j'apprenne en 1956,
huit ans après notre nuit,
qu'elle mourut dans une rue de Paris
quand une voiture venue par derrière
l'écrasa. Dans sa tombe
nous sommes assis à l'étroit
et nos causeries ne viennent jamais
à manquer de gravité.
En descendant du train du temps
(je pisse sur le temps), nous survivons tels des âmes
et nous sommes nos scandales
sur le quai en nous embrassant.

The Train to Paris

In the night boat train
from Le Havre to Paris
I sit by a young woman my age
who is from Carpentras,
daughter of a Breton sculptor
and we are heartsick
after our three hours. We know
we'll never meet again
but she will remember me,
our hands, and I her,
though I learn in 1956,
eight years after our night,
that she died on a Paris street
when a car crushed her
from behind. In her grave
we are sitting cramped
but our conversations never
run out of gravity.
Down from the train of time
(I piss on time), we endure as souls
and our scandals create us
on the platform kissing.

La belle nuit

La nuit de silence à tue-tête
dans un appartement glacial et austère
que j'aime assez. En haut la fin

des pas orageux d'un chat. Terminés
les pets des motocyclettes missionnaires
en bas sur Monsieur de Prince.

La rue sombre et charmante a le trac.
Il faut dormir mais pas de chance.
Je t'aperçois, je te transforme

d'un antique vers japonais.
Une fille de la rue apparaît.
Fin de l'histoire. Donc heureux je sors.

Dehors l'hiver. Il y a des froids
à traverser. La neige est belle
et j'oublie que termine la nuit.

The Beautiful Night

The night of booming silence in
an apartment austere and freezing
that I like enough. Upstairs an end

to a cat's roaring steps. No more
blast of farts from missionary motorcycles
down below on Monsieur le Prince.

The somber charming street has stage fright.
I have to sleep, but no such luck.
I perceive you, I transform you

from an old Japanese verse.
A girl of the street appears.
End of story. Then happy I go out

into the winter. There is ice to cross.
The snow is beautiful
and I forget that night is ending.

L'éléphant du bois de Vincennes

Souvent quand je regarde un éléphant méditant
dans le zoo, superbe de santé, me regardant
comme un grêle animal emprisonné dans la cage colossale
        en dehors de ses barreaux,

je songe au lointain cosmos invisible des lecteurs
qui me guettent ou ne me guettent point.
L'éléphant, gros et d'un cerveau énorme, est beau
        et d'une sagesse biblique,

un peu lourde. Il est mon juge. Je dépends de lui
pour mon alimentation, alors je fréquente l'habitat
où cet animal passe la nuit de solitude, à lire l'œuvre
        de ses visiteurs du jour.

Il me lira peut-être, si quelqu'un me le présente,
mais je fais mon pèlerinage au parc même quand il dort
pour l'étudier avec crainte et amour
        car je l'aime et le préfère

au magistrat humain de mes paroles. Je pense à l'éléphant,
ce monstre visible de jour, sans pages dans sa trompe
mais équipé de grands yeux astucieux
        pour déchiffrer la triste

éternité de ces gros livres qui font chier. N'ayant la force
de distinguer les perles de la merde (ou pire leur mélange)
dans mes strophes, je m'abandonne à lui, le muet,
        le bon mammouth.

The Elephant in the Bois de Vincennes

Often when I look at an elephant meditating
in the zoo, in superb health, and looking at me
as a spindly animal imprisoned in the colossal cage
                    outside his bars,

I daydream of a far invisible cosmos of readers
who look or do not look at me at all. The elephant,
huge and with his enormous brain, beauty and biblical
                    wisdom, is a little heavy

and my judge. I depend on him for my animus,
and I frequent the habitat where this animal spends
the night of solitude, reading the oeuvre
                    of his day visitors.

He may read me maybe, if someone introduces me to him,
and I make my pilgrimage to the park, even when
he is sleeping, to study him with dread and love,
                    since I like and prefer him

to the human magistrate of my words. I see the elephant,
this monster visible by day, carrying no pages
in his trunk, but outfitted with great astute eyes
                    to decipher the sad

eternity of boring books. I have no force
to tell the pearls from the shit (or worse their mixture)
in my verse, but I surrender to him the mute,
                    the good mammoth.

Le temps a laissé son manteau

pour Mort et Jeannette
sur la lune de la Seine

Le temps a laissé son manteau
et nous mangeons sur un bateau.
Quand j'étais pauvre à la Sorbonne
je flânais dans un Paris gris.
Mon bon copain Apollinaire
était un mot de joie et de pluie.
Le temps a gâché son manteau
mais nous causons sur un bateau.

Mangeant à l'École des Mines,
on dévalait deux mille pas
pour dévorer un repas noir
que seul un clochard aimerait.
Étant pauvre je l'aimais bien,
et j'ai trouvé le beau soleil
dans l'éclair blanc d'une souris.
Le temps a rongé son manteau.

Les nuits je ronflais dans un lit
de draps trop courts, et sous la pluie
la cour de l'hôtel puait l'urine.
Le temps s'en va mais je demeure.
Je suis maintenant fou et vieux,
les cheveux blancs du deuil de ma
jeunesse et du bon temps perdu,
mais nous jouissons sur un bateau.

Tout près sous le pont Mirabeau
dort la Seine d'amour perdu
et je dors dans un hôtel doux
(jadis je n'y serais entré).

Time Left Behind Her Winter Coat

for Mort and Jeannette
on the moon of the Seine

Time left behind her winter coat
and we are eating on a boat.
When I was poor at the Sorbonne
I strolled a Paris somber gray.
My cheerful pal Apollinaire
was a trench song of filthy rain.
Time has torn up her winter coat
and we are schmoozing on a boat.

Eating at the School of Mines,
I hopped down a thousand stairs
to slop up bowls of blackish grime
that only a hobo could bear,
but being broke I liked any lunch
and walked into beautiful sun
in the white lightning of a mouse.
Time has nibbled her winter coat.

Nights I was snoring in my bed
with sheets too short, and when it rained
the hotel courtyard stank of piss.
Time whimpers by but I hang on.
Now I'm a nut and not yet dead.
My hair is white in mourning for
my youth, a fat time now remote,
but we make love upon a boat.

Below the bridge of Mirabeau
slumbers a Seine of vanished love,
and I am sleeping in a sweet hotel
where once I never would dare go.

Pardonne mes erreurs lunaires.
J'aime causer avec les fleurs.
Le temps a brûlé son manteau
et nous buvons sur un bateau.

Paris, le 15 août 2000

So please forget my lunar errors.
I like to gossip with the flowers.
Time has burned up her winter coat
and we are drinking on a boat.

Paris, September 15, 1948

La rue Jacob, 1948

La guerre était la bombe pour Apollinaire
qui envoyait ses lettres-poèmes des tranchées.
Un obus peigna ses cheveux dans un éclair
mais Guillaume à Paris guérit enjoué
avec une cigarette aux lèvres comme une
ballade d'amour. Moi, j'espionnais la vie
de ma chambre d'hôtel, rouge le tapis,
l'eau chaude dans le lavabo, au coin la lune
sur nous. Je soupirais ravi quand les chanteurs
des rues attrapaient la grêle des sous. La cour
puait fumée de pisse quand la pluie du soir
tombait des nuages bleus de vin. Nos draps trop courts.
La grippe ravit le poète. Nous fûmes fous de bonheur
comme Gui qui creva le Jour de la Victoire.

La rue Jacob, 1948

War was fun for Guillaume Apollinaire,
sending letter poems from the trenches, yet
a bombshell came, gravely combing his hair,
but Guillaume healed in Paris, a cigarette
like a love ballad in his lips. I spied
life from a hotel room with a red rug,
hot water in the corner sink, and sighed
happy when the street singers used a jug
to catch the hailing francs. The courtyard reeked
with rising fumes of piss when evening rain
fell from the wine-blue clouds. Our sheets were far
too short. Fin de la guerre. Spanish flu creaked
into the poet's brain. We were young, zan-
y like Guillaume who croaked with La Victoire.

Je n'aime pas Paris

Je n'aime pas Paris. Peut-être
c'est la pluie bleue et j'hume le sel
quand les égouts chantent leurs cris
de troglodytes. J'aime Paris.

C'est le soleil de trois bleuets
qui chuchotent que mes papiers
sont faux, que j'habite une chambre
sur Cherche-Midi. Le concierge

tous les soirs porte une chatte noire
sur son épaule. Sans blague.
Il rit sévère et moi j'ai peur.
Néanmoins un bleu premier juin

bleu sur la Place Saint Sulpice,
le sixième arrondissement,
je me marie à la mairie,
mais je perds la clé. Pas de chambre,

donc nous dormons chez elle. «Qui est
ce gosse avec qui vous avez
passé la nuit?» dit la matrone.
«C'est mon mari.» Elle nous jette

dans la rue. Je n'aime pas
Paris. Je l'aime tendrement,
tous les artistes qui crèvent,
la pluie sale, le soleil bleu.

I Don't Love Paris

I don't love Paris. Maybe
it's the blue rain and I smell salt
when the sewers sing their cries
of the troglodyte. I love Paris.

It's the sun of three bluets
who whisper that my papers
are fake and I live in a room
on Cherche-Midi. The concierge

each night holds a black cat
on his shoulder. No kidding.
He laughs tersely and I am scared.
Nonetheless a blue first of June

blue on la Place Saint Sulpice,
in the sixth arrondissement,
I marry in the city hall
but I lose my key. No room,

we sleep at her place. "Who is
this boy with whom you've spent
the night?" says the landlady.
"He's my husband." She throws us

into the street. I don't like
Paris. I love her tenderly,
her one-room starving artists,
the dirty rain, the blue sun.

Le lit, la classe de philo, et Paul Verlaine

Le lit ést nu. Une couverture
rouge, déchirée sous une ampoule de trente watts
peut-être, si je peux compter,
crachotant haute sur le plafond, clignant d'œil à mes caleçons
ridés mouillés gouttant lentement sur le bord
du lavabo. Je m'habille et sors.

Le matin un soleil dans sa
chaussette décousue, je marche vers ma dure classe de philo
sur Auguste Compte. Je ne dis
rien mais je jouis de la brillance des débats entre étudiants
et le bon prof M. La Porte.
Un jour j'arrive. Le professeur

est tombé mort. Griffonné
sur un morceau de papier morne, joyeusement cloué à la porte,
un avis: *La Porte est fermée.*
Un ami espagnol me voit déçu et m'offre un livre rare
du surréaliste Aleixandre,
Épées Comme Lèvres, qui un jour

me guidera à une porte à Madrid.
Nous bavardons sur Miguel Hernández, sa lumière, mort en prison.
Puis en rentrant chez moi, je passe
par la sombre rue de Prince, un petit hôtel où le prince
Paul Verlaine un bon soir s'allongea
saturé et mort sur le plancher.

Bed, Philosophy Class, and Paul Verlaine

The bed is bare. A red
torn blanket below a bulb of maybe thirty watts,
    if I can count,
sputtering high on the ceiling, winking at my wet wrinkled underwear
    dripping slowly onto the edge
    of the sink. I dress and go out.

The morning, a sun in her
ragged sock, I walk to my tough philosophy class
    on Auguste Compte. I say nothing
but enjoy the fierce flashing debates between students
    and the good prof Monsieur La Porte.
    One day I arrive. The professor

had fallen dead. Scrawled
on a piece of bleak paper gleefully tacked to the door,
    a notice: *La Porte est fermée.*
A Spanish friend sees me let down and gives me a rare book
    of the surrealist Aleixandre,
    Swords like Lips that one day

will guide me to a door in Madrid.
We chat about Miguel Hernández, his light, his death in prison.
    Returning home I scurry along
the somber rue de Prince, a little hotel where the prince
    Paul Verlaine one good evening lay down,
    soaking drunk and dead on the floor.

À la Sorbonne lisait Paul Éluard à la foule

Parmi la foule devant la Sorbonne
    j'avais de dégoûtantes manières.
        Un flic en noir

fixa son regard sévère sur moi
    et me demanda non sans grâce
        de circuler.

Je répondis en marchant sur son pied.
    Le flic se recula blessé,
        criant: «*Monsieur!*»

La misère. J'étais un vrai cochon.
    De '48 je garde encore
        ce souvenir

comme si j'avais pissé sur la France.
    La foi dans la salle pour
        Le Rassemblement

des Intellectuels Contre le Fascisme
    brûlait et Louis Aragon
        dirigeait.

Assis sur la scène à côté d'Eluard
    un prêtre, fusil sur les genoux,
        écoutait.

Éluard lisait les noms des mineurs tués
    dans une grève. Un silence.
        Le père cria:

«*S'il faut lutter, nous lutterons!*» Alors il
    sauta sur ses pieds, levant son fusil
        au plafond.

Apollinaire and Lorca

I live, I'm not one of the dead
like a malcontent poet
who in the thirty-eighth year of life
is wiped out by a microbe
or by four bullets of hatred

to cut off his neck of sun.
Our two comrades Apollinaire
and Lorca, two angels the age
of a boy, have gone inside
the box of absolute silence.

You hear them of course, but nothing
after their thirty-eighth year,
and only their shadow in ink.
I want their words singing below
the sky below the black earth,

apocryphal but in the heart.
I am a lucky one. I've almost
the years of those two together
in their young death. I breathe,
counting the raspberry kisses.

I sit down, write, tell them thanks
for the cunning of their grace
in drinking the iris of the moon.
A pigeon cannot fathom its flight,
the wind doesn't get it. They carry

song like clouds slipping sideways
like crabs tumbling into the unknown.
Our two comrades Apollinaire
and Lorca, two angels of a too
stingy age, inhabit the white
box of death as they mumble love.

Le pont Mirabeau

Sous le pont Mirabeau coule la Seine
Et nos amours
Faut-il qu'il m'en souvienne
La joie venait toujours après la peine

Vienne la nuit sonne l'heure
Les jours s'en vont je demeure

Les mains dans les mains restons face à face
Tandis que sous
Le pont de nos bras passe
Des éternels regards l'onde si lasse

Vienne la nuit sonne l'heure
Les jours s'en vont je demeure

L'amour s'en va comme cette eau courante
L'amour s'en va
Comme la vie est lente
Et comme l'Espérance est violente

Vienne la nuit sonne l'heure
Les jours s'en vont je demeure

Passent les jours et passent les semaines
Ni temps passé
Ni les amours reviennent
Sous le pont Mirabeau coule la Seine

Vienne la nuit sonne l'heure
Les jours s'en vont je demeure

Guillaume Apollinaire

The Bridge Mirabeau

Below the bridge Mirabeau flows the Seine
              And our loves
           Must I recall again
That joy came always after pain

       Comes the night the hour tolls
       The days withdraw I remain

Let us stand face to face hands in our hands
            while below the bridge
         Of our arms pass the bands
Of waves weary in their eternal glance

       Comes the night the hour tolls
       The days withdraw I remain

Our love goes by like this meandering flow
            Our love withdraws
         As life is slow
And Hope gives out a violent blow

       Comes the night the hour tolls
       The days withdraw I remain

The days and weeks pass by cannot remain
            And neither past
         Nor loves return again
Below the bridge Mirabeau flows the Seine

       Comes the night the hour tolls
       The days withdraw I remain

                    Guillaume Apollinaire

Nuit de l'Île du Diable

Je suis un voyou et je ne pense
à rien sauf au vinaigre dans mon âme.
Le soir le plus blême d'un Paris sale,

j'éclaire les bancs d'hilarité des Halles
par une soupe à l'oignon, et je partage
mon petit déjeuner avec un voleur libéré

depuis peu de l'Île du Diable.
Le bon voleur me montre ses papiers juste avant
de me piller. Alors je prends le métro,

passe par une douche publique, et change le peu
de dollars qui me restent dans la poche
au marché noir. Un ami joue de l'harmonica

qu'il fixe sur sa guitare et chante
en un russe inventé qui me rend dingue.
Je décampe du café sûr comme le cul d'un chameau.

J'échange mes souliers contre des ailes
et flotte, un faucon au dessus de la frontière,
cherchant un jeu de dés avec quelques anges.

Night of Devil's Island

I am a rascal and I ponder only
on nothing except the vinegar in my soul.
Evening, the palest of a dirty Paris,

I light up the benches of hilarity at Les Halles
with an onion soup, and I share
my small breakfast with a thief discharged

a while ago from Devil's Island.
The good thief shows me his papers just before
pillaging me. Then I take the metro

to a public shower and change a few
of the lonely dollars in my pocket
on the black market. A friend plays the harmonica

that he sets up on his guitar, and sings
in invented Russian that drives me wacky.
I take off from the café, safe as a camel's ass.

Then I change shoes for wings and float,
a falcon high over the border,
looking for a crap game with a few angels.

L'Après-midi d'un cerf

C'est bon de coucher à Paris quand on a vingt ans,
en face du Jardin du Luxembourg dans l'Hôtel
      de Lisbonne et Portugal.

Je marchais partout. On avait besoin des pieds,
c'est tout. Les noms des ruelles et des cafés
      étaient alors des cœurs

lunaires imprimés dans une tasse noire
de chocolat amer. À l'étage au-dessus
      dormait mon premier ami

écrivain. C'était Bernard Frechtman, traducteur
et poète. Il lut mes vers, me prit au sérieux,
      et dès lors je me sentis

membre de ce gang de gitans se cachant
sous tous les tapis du monde, songeant à l'Est,
      pour leur repas de soleil.

Il venait de traduire *Notre-Dame des Fleurs,*
et un soir Bernard descendu me montrer
      des photos de Jean Genet.

J'ai dis que Genet avait une belle gueule
rappante. Point final. Alors il me raconta l'histoire
      de Sartre et du directeur

de la prison qui conspiraient. Sartre voulait
envoyer des livres à Genet. Mais pour donner
      au voleur un peu de plaisir,

The Afternoon of a Deer

Good to sleep in Paris when one is twenty,
in front of the Luxembourg Garden in the Hotel
      of Lisbon and Portugal.

I walked everywhere. You needed feet,
that's all. The names of alleys and cafés
      then became lunar

hearts printed in a black cup
of bitter chocolate. Up on the third floor
      slept my first writer

friend. It was Bernard Frechtman, translator
and poet. He read my verse, took me seriously
      and from then on I felt

a member of that gang of gypsies hiding
under every rug in the world, dreaming East
      for a meal of sun.

He'd just translated *Our Lady of the Flowers*,
and one evening Bernard came down to show me
      some photos of Jean Genet.

I said that Genet had a striking and handsome
mug. Period. Then he told me a story
      of Sartre and the prison

warden who were conspiring. Sartre wanted
to send Genet some books. But to get them
      to the thief with some fun

le directeur plaça les cadeaux sur les rayons
de la bibliothèque et en fit de Genet leur gardien.
        Ainsi il pouvait piquer

les romans et nager dans l'acte de les lire.
Le lendemain soir Bernard était à la porte,
        tout souriant. «Qu'est-ce qu'il y a?»

«Je viens de sa cellule. Genet est ému.»
«Pourquoi?» «C'est simple. Il est heureux» me dit-il,
        «car un jeune écrivain

américain trouve que ce voleur commun
est beau.» Un après-midi je me reposais
        sur mon couvre-lit rouge

quand quelqu'un frappa. J'eus du mal à ouvrir,
Je m'étais fait une entorse à la cheville. Puis,
        rien. Kathy entra. Moi,

poète? Oui. Depuis une année. Une chemise
de poésie. «Écoute, Willis. À New York je crois
        que je peux te trouver

un éditeur pour ton livret.» J'ai commencé
à bondir sur le lit, un cerf d'un seul pied.
        Après avoir quitté la France

j'échangeais des lettres avec Bernard. Un ami
qui fabriquait l'espoir. Et après cinq ans, silence.
        Alors je suis revenu.

the warden placed the gifts on the library
shelves and made Genet their guardian
          so he could swipe

the novels and swim in the act of reading them.
The next evening Bernard was at the door,
          all smiles. "What's up?"

I've just come from his cell. Genet is moved."
"Why?" "It's simple. He's happy," he told me.
          that a young America writer

finds this common thief handsome.
One afternoon I'm out of it, dozing
          on the red bedspread,

someone knocks. I had trouble opening
having just sprained my ankle. Time
          hanging. Kathy came in.

Me a poet? Yes, as of one year. A folder
of verse. "Listen, Willis. I think I can find you
          a New York publisher

to bring out a small book." I began
to bounce on the bed, a one-footed deer.
          When I left France

I exchanged letters with Bernard. A friend
who invented hope. After five years, silence.
          Then I came back.

Frechtman n'habitait plus la chambre d'amitié.
Un camarade enfin décrivit sa torpeur,
      sa dépression après

avoir rompu avec son amante de longtemps.
«Et puis?» Bernard trouva une corde et se pendit
      au-dessus de l'escalier

de l'Hôtel de Lisbonne et Portugal en face
du Jardin, et sans le miracle de la rose
      le bon voleur s'échappa.

Frechtman no longer had that room of friendship.
A guy I knew finally described his stupor,
        the depression after

he and his longtime girlfriend split. "Then?"
Bernard found a rope and hanged himself
        over the staircase

of the Hotel of Lisbon and Portugal facing
the Garden, and with no miracle of the rose
        the good thief escaped.

L'après-midi dans une Léproserie, 1960

Une vision de la renaissance se vantait
des démons du péché dans la folie,
mais pendant le haut moyen âge le succès
fou partout était les léproseries,

des milliers de lazarets pour bien séparer
les infectieux du diable qui s'accroupissent
abominables sur leurs mains et sur leurs pieds.
Il n'y en a que dix millions aujourd'hui

grâce à la sulfone qui peut régénérer
souvent les lésions et même la pluie
de bacilles nageant dans le sang. Un seul
après-midi avec les lépreux, la colonie

dominait la colline sur la mer. Il y avait
Leopold en haut qui avait refroidi
son cousin Bobbie Franks de Chicago, l'année
'24. Trente-six ans plus tard, sorti

de prison, comme pénitence il se trouvait
avec 27 pestiférés. On sourit
à mon arrivée. Leopold courtaud, ballonné
dans sa jaquette blanche, prit

ma main et nous bavardâmes toute la journée.
Le diable était humain. Son grand hobby
était les oiseaux. Autrefois le crime parfait
et les mathématiques tous deux abolis

Afternoon in the Colony, 1960

One vision of the renaissance brags
of demons of sin in madness,
but during the late middle ages the wild hit
every place was leper colonies,

millions of leprosariums to insulate
those infected with the devil, who crawled
abominably on their hands and knees.
There are only ten million today

thanks to sulfur drugs that often can
regenerate lesions and even the rain
of bacilli swimming in the blood. Just one
afternoon with lepers. The colony

commanded the hill over the sea. There was
Leopold up there who had iced
his cousin Bobbie Franks from Chicago, in
'24. Thirty-six years later, released

from the pen, for his penitence he lived among
the pestiferous. They smiled
when I got there. Short Leopold, ballooning
in his white jacket, took

my hand and we blabbed all day long.
The devil was human. His grand hobby
was birds. Earlier the perfect crime
and mathematics, all abolished now

pour guérir les corps des mourants. Chauve, en paix
et méticuleux, Nathan, sa vie
isolée dans l'air ensoleillé qui durerait
encore sept ans, me rendit heureux, m'instruisit

sur la santé. J'avais senti le vent fêlé
de la folie, mais ce rondelet de Leopold,
assassin d'un adolescent oublié
à ce jour, soulageait les lépreux maudits.

to heal the bodies of the dying. Bald, in peace
and meticulous, Nathan, now in an isolated
life with seven years left in the sun-filled air,
cheered me, instructed me

about health. I had heard the cracked wind
of madness, but this roly-poly
Leopold, assassin of an adolescent forgotten to
our day, comforted the cursed lepers.

Dans un faubourg de Paris

Mon amie polonaise à la Sorbonne grise
aime le poète espagnol Bécquer. Amusante,
mince comme Chopin, dans ses laines pesantes
une nuit de pluie en secret elle me conduit
à une fête sombre de l'Armée de la Pologne
Libre dans une pièce orange, au deuxième
étage. Nous sommes des camarades, même
en marchant sous les bannières, Bois de Boulogne.
De grand cœur et chaleureuse au lit,
mardi matin nous quittons Paris. Elle prend
ma main. Une maison louche dans un faubourg.
Je n'en sais rien. «Je suis enceinte. L'avortement
en France est défendu.» Le charlatan de morgue
coupe: «Voilà votre chef-d'œuvre.» On est pourri.

In a Paris Faubourg

My Polish classmate at the gray Sorbonne
loves the romantic poet Bécquer. She
wears heavy wool, is Chopin-thin and fun
in Paris rain. One night she secrets me
off to a grim Free Polish Army party
up in an orange room. We're comrades and
march behind banners down Boule Miche. Hearty
and generous in bed, she takes my hand
a Sunday morning; we go to a faubourg,
a sleazy house. I don't guess why. "It's clear,"
she says. "I'm pregnant and abortion's not
a legal act in France." Up in the morgue
the foreign doctor cuts her up. "So, here
is your chef-d'oeuvre," he tells me. I am rot.

Chant des oiseaux

Après l'enregistrement de Pablo Casals
Ell ocells, en haut sur le Canigo[3],
nous allâmes à pied de la vieille chapelle à
la montagne sous un tapis d'astres jusqu' au manteau
de blé doux en bas. On ne voyait rien. Tu tenais
ma main car la pente était raide. Puis sur
l'herbe nous nous vîmes. Nus. Comme l'ordonnait
l'âme naturelle, nous nous allongeâmes jeunes, sûrs
de notre sang. Nos langues étaient d'eau, nos yeux
énormes, la terre un feu inconnu jusqu'à l'aube,
des vaches et les braillants enfants d'un village
nous reconduisirent. Je t'adorais dans notre alpage
contre la loi. La nuit était soleil. Je rôde
muet, mais notre montagne est un fil lumineux.

[3] El cant del ocells. Le chant des oiseaux (du catalan). La chanson etait composee par le violoncelliste Pablo Casals.

Song of the Birds

After Pablo Casals had taped *The Song
of the Birds*, high on Canigo[4], we went
by foot, from the old French convent, along
the mountain rug of stars, down to the scent
of wheat. We couldn't see. You held my hand
because the trail was steep. Then in the grove
we saw ourselves. Naked. By the command
of natural soul, we lay down young and drove
our blood. Our tongues were water, our eyes huge,
earth an unknowing fire until the dawn
of cows and village children screaming led
us back. I loved you in our pure refuge
against the law. The night was sun. Though gone,
our virgin mountain is a lucent thread.

---

[4] El cant del ocells. The song of the birds (from Catalan). The song was composed by
the cellist Pablo Casals.

La folie de lire la vie de quelqu'un

Si tu possèdes la folie de lire ma vie,
je te la donne froide. Un œuf à l'aube
vaut plus qu'un gros bifteck à minuit.
Je m'égare, les yeux étoiles. Le paysage silencieux

est un maître criard. Le désert du Sinaï soupire
tant que notre Jeep regarde la montagne. Je la grimpe
et le sable se change en roc et cloche de monastère,
et j'entends un chuchotement vert dans le Vermont.

Rilke était assis, vêtu impeccable et solitaire
dans son château de pierre glaciale en février
et sur son bureau solide il inventa Orphée.
Nous sommes beaucoup, les disciplinés en folie.

En Chine j'ai suivi la Route de la Soie des caravanes,
perles de rivière, menthe et safran sur les charrettes
bon marché du ventre de l'Asie, et moi,
un dragoman, un vagabond rempli d'esprit,

et rentrant en Grèce je brûle avec des images
d'icônes d'îles aussi brisées que le peu de colonnes
sur la plaine d'Olympie. Lis ma vie
dans une solitude de bureau de minuit

par laquelle j'aime être épuisé. J'espère habiter
l'escalier de l'eau. Je me nourris de mes échecs
sur ces savanes d'isolement. Clairement un crétin.
Tu dis que je délire, mais je fais

The Folly of Reading Somebody's Life

If you have the folly to read my life,
I hand it to you cold. An egg at dawn
is better than a fat midnight steak.
I walk around, my eyes stars. The silent landscape

is a screaming master. The Sinai desert
sighs as our jeep sights the mountain. Then I climb up
as sand turns to rock and a monastery bell,
and I hear a green whisper in Vermont.

Rilke sat impeccably dressed and alone
in his freezing stone chateau in February
and on his heavy desk he invented Orpheus.
We are many, the disciplined in madness.

In China I followed the Silk Road of caravans,
river pearls, mint et saffron on the carts,
cheap in the stomach of Asia, and I
a dragoman, a vagabond full of spirit,

and back in Greece I burn with images
of island icons as broken as the few standing columns
on the Olympian plain. Read my life
in a midnight office loneliness

I love to be exhausted by. I hope to inhabit
the stairway of water. I feed on failures
in these prairies of isolation. Clearly a cretin.
You say I'm losing my mind,

l'amour dans la pluie avec des cuisses chantantes
dans notre pré isolé piqué par les acacias
et je joue dans la neige rosée de tes bras.
Après nous nous asseyons sur un banc, regardons le sourcil

du soir descendant sur nos côtes. Si tu as
la amabilité de lire ma vie, je l'étoile sur un verre. Regarde
la transparence. Un mensonge parfait.
Dis-moi, si je dois dégringoler dans le noir.

but I make love in rain with chanting thighs
in our isolated meadow prickled with acacia trees
and play in the pink snow of your arms.
After that we sit on a bench and look at the eyebrow

of the evening descending to our ribs.
If you have the kindness to read my life, I craze it
on glass. Look through it. A perfect lie.
Tell me if I should hurdle into the black.

Parmi les orphelins

Je suis un simple soldat d'après-guerre
ici à Périgueux, un centre gastronomique
    avec truffes de cochon.

L'église byzantine médite loin
de sa mère à Constantinople.
    Ses mosaïques

ont des figures incorporelles, des têtes
et des yeux énormément grecs,
    pénétrant les murailles,

et moi qui ne fous rien dans la ville
sinon tourner les pages de bons romans
    de Colette.

Je ne suis pas un bon soldat, pas propre,
avec le seul devoir d'asseoir mon cul
    sur la table ou jouer

à l'interprète quand un de mes complices
tombe le nez dans la boue après une connerie
    érotique. Je cause

avec les flics qui l'ont arrêté, et souvent
on le libère parce qu'on veut demander
    à cette énigme que je suis,

mon avis sur les orphelins, et pourquoi
je leur rends visite à l'asile et à l'hôpital
    des nonnes juste hors de la ville.

Among the Orphans

I'm an after-the-war soldier stationed
at Périgueux, a gastronomic center
      with pig truffles.

The Byzantine church meditates far
from the mother at Constantinople.
      Her mosaics

have incorporeal faces with enormously
Greek heads and almond eyes penetrating
      the walls and me

with nothing to do in the city but go
to a café or meadow and turn pages
      of Colette's novels.

I'm not a good soldier, spit-polish clean.
My sole duty is to sit my ass on my desk
      or play interpreter

when a buddy lands flat in the mud
after an erotic stupidity.
      I chat with the arresting flics

and often they let the offender go
since they like to question me, an
      enigma. What is it

with the orphans? Why do I visit them
in the asylum and the nuns' hospital just
      outside of town?

Les nonnes gracieuses ne sont pas ennemies
sans-cœur de Jean Gabin ou Louis Jouvet.
            Certainement aveugle,

je rentre au camp sur l'avenue Joseph Staline,
un nom créé avec esprit pour la ruelle
            de notre caserne.

Parmi les miens je suis un étranger.
Le week-end j'aime me perdre tout près
            dans un village

rougeâtre et brun, puant l'urine et la vieillesse,
où l'essayiste Michel de Montaigne
            dans sa retraite rit et marche

dans les champs herbeux de rêves défiants.
Ses pensées dessinent une montagne latine
            prouvant que quand on regarde

on ne voit rien. Le rire d'une Juive portugaise,
sa mère, lui donne la force de mourir jeune,
            trop jeune comme

nous. Il peint le Périgord de sa perception
douce verte, et moi, ce soldat vagabond,
            arrivé parmi les orphelins,

les flics, Colette et Michel de Montaigne,
je ne peux quitter ce centre de truffes
            et de gastronomie.

The gracious nuns are not heartless enemies
of actors like Jean Gabin or Louis Jouvet.
        Definitely blind,

I go back to our camp on l'avenue Joseph Stalin,
a name wittily created for the alley
        of our barracks.

Among my own I am a foreigner.
On weekends I like to get lost very near
        in a village reddish

and brown, stinking of urine and age,
where the essayist Michel de Montaigne
        in his retreat laughs

and walks grassy fields of defiant dreams.
His thought draws a Latin mountain to prove
        when we look we see

nothing. His laugh comes from a Portuguese Jew,
his mother who gives him the strength to die
        young, too young,

like us. He paints the Périgord in soft green
perception, while I, this vagrant soldier,
        come among orphans,

les flics, Colette and Michel de Montaigne,
cannot leave this center of pig truffles
        and gastronomy.

Soldat de la paix

J'étais soldat, le bel automne de paix.
Vif! Oh personne n'avait peur de nous.
On n'entendait plus les obus siffler.
Les morts debout dans les tranchées
Devient des amants couchés dans leur trous.

L'Adieu

J'ai cueilli ce brin de bruyère
L'automne est mort souviens-t'en
Nous ne nous verrons plus sur terre
Odeur du temps brin de bruyère
Et souviens-toi que je t'attends

Guillaume Apollinaire

Soldier of the Peace

I was a soldier, peace in the sweet fall.
Wow! Oh no one was afraid of us.
No longer did I hear the bombshells fall,
and the dead men standing in the trenches
turned into lovers sleeping in their hole.

The Farewell

I picked this sprig of heather
Autumn is dead recall our fate
On earth we'll never see each other
Smell of time sprig of heather
And remember for you I wait

Guillaume Apollinaire

La tour Eiffel

> Bergère ô tour Eiffel le troupeau des ponts bêle ce matin
>
> —Guillaume Apollinaire

Sous la tour Eiffel bavardent Paris
    et ma jeunesse.
Pourquoi ai-je attendu une demi-vie
    pour sa tendresse?

Première nuit à la gare du Nord
    à un bar de zinc,
je bus un café noir et deux cognacs
    mais où coucher?

C'était la grève et aucun autobus
    gênant la pluie.
Trempé, perdu, j'ai dormi dans la rue
    comme une goutte

de bonheur. Qui pouvait rouspéter contre
    un émigrant
de foi? La guerre à peine finie mais
    colique, colère

et l' art dans l'air, les ailes des flics, les marches
    de '48.
«Je pisse sur de Gaulle,» cria un jeune type
    sur la statue

devant La Comédie. *«Bien, pissez donc!»*
    hurla la foule,
et un arc-en-ciel jaune illumina
    le noir de la nuit.

Below the Eiffel Tower

Shepherd O Eiffel Tower the troop of bridges love this morning

—Guillaume Apollinaire

Below the Eiffel Tower Paris gossips
    and my youth too.
Why have I waited half a life
    for her tenderness?

First evening at the Gare du Nord
    at a bar of zinc,
I drank black coffee and two cognacs
    but where to sleep?

There was a strike and no buses
    bothered the rain.
Drenched, lost, I slept in the street
    like a drop

of happiness. Who could quarrel with
    an emigrant
of faith? The war barely over but
    colic, anger

and art in the air, the wings of cops,
    the marches, '48.
"*I piss on de Gaulle,*" cried a young guy
    atop the statue

in front of the Comédie. "*Okay, piss away!*"
    the mob yelled,
and a yellow rainbow illuminated
    the black of night.

Sous la tour Eiffel palabrent Paris
        et mes échecs gais.
Pourquoi ai-je attendu une demi-vie
        pour y revenir?

Sous la tour les kiosques de Saint-Germain,
        rafraîchissent
le matin du *Figaro, Herald, Monde*
        et moi le Juif

errant, non pas le Juif mais l'étranger
        qui parle bien
la belle langue quand il peut oublier
        qu'il n'y entend rien

du tout. J'aime Paris, les putes du
        bon Baudelaire
et l'aube d'été et l'acier de Rimbaud,
        mes deux intimes

avant le déluge. Mais des problèmes.
        Je ne m'aime pas
moi-même. L'esprit d'escalier, c'est moi
        et je languis

pour les belles laides que je n'ai pas
        embrassées. L'âme
pourrie toujours, un homme de regret,
        je lutte mal

pour un narcisse de paix, un jardin
        de la colombe,
un asphodèle près de mon hôtel
        de rêves, chambre

Below the Eiffel Tower chats Paris
and my light fiascos.
Why have I waited half my life
just to be back?

Under the tower the kiosks of Saint-Germain,
are refreshing
the morning of *Figaro, Herald, Monde,*
and me the wandering

Jew and not the Jew but foreigner
who talks nicely
in the beautiful tongue when he forgets
he knows nothing

about it. I love Paris, the whores
of Baudelaire,
the dawn of sun and ice of Rimbaud,
my two intimates

before the flood. But some troubles.
I don't care for
me. The spirit of the stairway is me
and I languish

for the lovely disasters I haven't
kissed. Always
a rotten soul, a man of regret,
I fight poorly

for a narcissus of peace, a garden
of the dove,
an asphodel near my hotel
of dreams, room

cauchemar. La nuit sur ma tête s'éveille
la tour Eiffel
étoilée et chante sur la fenêtre
de mon atelier.

Sous la tour Eiffel somnolent les ponts.
Ils bouffent des brioches.
Les avions mettent leurs lunettes. Ils grognent:
«Le temps est moche.»

Mais dans la Brasserie du Marché loin
des prix d'enfer,
je ne regrette rien. Je suis ici
respirant du cœur.

Sous la tour Eiffel s'amuse Paris
et ma jeunesse.
Pourquoi est-j'ai attendu une demi-vie
pour sa tendresse?

of nightmare. Night on my head wakens
		the Eiffel Tower
starry and singing on the window
		of my atelier.

Below the Eiffel Tower the bridges sleep.
		They wolf brioches.
Airplanes put on their glasses. They groan,
		"The weather stinks,"

but in the Brasserie of the Market, far
		from infernal prices,
I've nothing to regret. I'm here,
		breathing heart.

Below the Eiffel Tower Paris is funny
		and my youth too.
Why have I waited half a life
		for her tenderness?

Parfums de la Sorbonne

Cet après-midi il fait si beau.
Le soleil est un abricot
dans ma poche qui chauffe bien
malgré l'hiver et mon chagrin.

J'ai parcouru les vieilles ruelles
de ma jeunesse et le bateau
de fous et fumistes fidèles
à la brume et le soleil gros

dans le cartable d'écolier,
et j'y étudiais avec Delattre
le prof brillant qui refusait
de laisser une Juive—quatre

ans plus tôt—être dans la classe
pour présenter son doctorat
sur John Keats. Il manqua de grâce.
Hélène Berr juste rata

de deux jours à Bergen-Belsen
la libération. Le typhus
lui légua son diplôme de peine,
son *Journal*, son âme dans l'opus

brillant de feu. L'après-midi est si beau.
Le soleil est un abricot
dans ma poche qui chauffe bien
malgré l'hiver et mon chagrin.

                              Paris, 1948-2008

Aromas of the Sorbonne

This afternoon is beautiful
and the sun is an apricot
in my pocket, heating well
against winter and my upset.

I went back to the small alleys
of my young days and to the ship
of fools and wisecrackers who pleased
the fog and heavy sun that slipped

into my schoolbag as I cruised
the maize. I studied with Delattre,
the brilliant prof who refused
to let a Jew–four years earlier–

remain a student in his class
and to present her doctorate
on John Keats. The prof lacked grace.
Hélène Berr, locked in the camp

lacked just two days in Bergen-Belsen
from liberation, but camp typhus
bequeathed her a degree in pain,
her *Journal*, her soul in an opus

of flame. Afternoon is beautiful
and sun remains an apricot
in my pocket, heating well
against winter and my regret.

                    Paris, 1948-2008

Les yeux de Dieu

Je ne songe jamais aux yeux de Dieu
qui ne chuchote pas son éclair dans le repos
      de mon fantôme aveugle,
      et je me fous

de ses pâtures vertes flottant sur les nuages
où Dieu garde son domaine de harpistes
      et un conflit d'anges.
      La syphilis morne,

qui tua Schubert, ne peut pas me toucher.
Nous possédons de nos jours de fortes antidotes.
      Je vis, ignorant
      les bras de la mort

qui n'a pas de maison, et je caresse l'ennui
et tombe follement dans la quête d'un gros vent
      pour m'emporter
      en Chine

vers une montagne sainte et à une chèvre
pour en nettoyer la cime. Enfin je suis une goutte
      de nuit, à peine
      une personne.

Quand je me sauverai, le firmament me ravira
impatient de déguster mon bol de vie.
      Le ciel, qui n'a pas
      de gorge, rit,

mais à quoi bon se fâcher contre un mur?
Donc, je ne hurle pas fort devant l'éternité,
      tant que les yeux
      de Dieu sont de verre.

The Eyes of God

I never daydream of the eyes of God
who cannot whisper lightning into the leisure
      of my blind ghost.
      I don't give a fuck

about her green meadows floating on clouds
where she watches her domain of harpists
      and a discord of angels.
      The torture of syphilis

that killed Schubert can't get to me.
In our century we have powerful antidotes.
      I live by snubbing
      the arms of death,

who is homeless, and hug boredom
and tumble crazy, looking for a fat wind
      to blow my frail
      boat into China,

to a holy mountain and a goat to clean up
that peak. Finally I am a drop of night,
      hardly a person.
      When I take off,

the firmament will ravish and choke me,
impatient to swallow my bowl of life.
      The sky has no throat
      yet she laughs.

What good is it to rage against a wall?
So I don't howl much before eternity
      as long as the eyes
      of God are glass.

Bonheur irrémédiable

pour Marianne et Frank

L'automne a trop d'hiver pour préserver l'automne.
Dans ma douche l'aube noircie et paresseuse
me confie qu'elle doute, donc elle brille. La bonne

planète naine tousse et offre ses lois fâcheuses.
L'automne a assez d'hiver. Dansant le faux automne,
étoile coupée, l'aube noire est voluptueuse.

Le chien de la forêt secrète toujours me protège,
grignotant l'ordure. Trempé, le bonheur m'étonne.
Toutes les saisons de l'aube hurlent leur cœur de neige.

L'automne a trop d'hiver pour préserver l'automne.

Incurable Happiness

for Marianne et Frank

Fall has too much winter to preserve fall.
In my shower the blackish and lazy dawn
confides her doubts in me and glows, the whole

good dwarf planet coughs, offers clumsy laws,
and autumn has enough of winter. False fall
dances. Black dawn, a severed star, is voluptuous,

the dog of the secret forest protects me now,
gnawing garbage. I'm drenched, stunned by joy. All
seasons of the dawn scream their heart of snow.

Fall has too much winter to preserve fall.

L'encre du bonheur

«Est-ce que j'ose manger une pêche?» écrivit
le jeune Eliot. Est-ce que j'ose
griffonner sur un écran ce patois

dormant au fond d'un souvenir
d'il y a mille ans. «Bill qu'es-tu devenu?»
Aujourd'hui je viens d'acheter

un dictionnaire. Les amants pharaoniques,
buvant de la bière sur le Nil,
respirent dans le livre de magie. Mon camarade

est l'espoir pour l'infini,
pour un ciel de bouquins circulant au-dessus
des yeux des éditeurs lunaires.

Ce soleil de mots est mon jus d'orange.
Merci. C'est frais. Il me libère.
Mes gaffes sans dents mais visibles sourient,

soupirent. Ne crains rien. Je m'en vais.
En attendant les cartes des planètes,
je danse dans l'encre du bonheur.

Ink of Joy

Do I dare to eat a peach? wrote the young
Eliot. And do I dare
to scribble on a screen this patois

sleeping at the bottom of a memory
of a thousand years ago. Bill, what've you become?
Hang on! Today I just bought

a dictionary. Pharaonic lovers drinking beer
on the Nile all breathe
in the book of magic. My comrade

is hope for the infinite,
for a sky of books circulating above
the eyes of lunar publishers.

This sunshine of words is my orange juice.
Thanks. It's fresh. It frees me
when my bloopers are toothless but visibly smile

and sigh. Don't be scared. I'm leaving.
While waiting for maps from the planets,
I dance in the ink of joy.

Lectrice, lecteur

Lectrice, lecteur invisible, je t'aime.
        Pourquoi gâches-tu
    tes soirs avec moi dans ton lit?

Ici j'ai quelques amis; personne comme toi.
        Je suis devenu
    le hibou qui calcule la nuit.

L'aurore me trouve écrasé. Tous ceux qui m'aiment
        je les loue. «Mon
    pauvre cœur est un hibou,»

se plaint Guillaume. Mais tu as prêté
        ta belle langue,
    à un étranger, à un vagabond

qui onze années circule et boit l'Europe.
        Tu seras déçue
    mais je me sens le bienvenu.

Je t'avais abandonnée, pourtant ma première
        poésie sortit
    dans une revue de Paris,

Les Points, un journal bilingue, la couverture
        jaune brilla
    dans tous les kiosques, et les bonnes

bourgeoises l'achetèrent comme du fromage,
        croyant acquérir
    une revue de tricot. L'éditeur,

Woman Reader, Man Reader

Woman reader, unseen man reader, I love you.
       Why do you waste
    your evenings with me in your bed?

Here I have a few friends, no one like you.
       I have become
    the owl calculating night.

Daybreak finds me crushed. All who love me
       I've rented. My
    poor heart is an owl,

Guillaume beefs. But you have lent
       your beautiful tongue
    to a stranger, a vagabond

of eleven years circulating in Europe.
       You'll be let down
    but I feel welcome.

I abandoned you, and yet my first
       poem came out
    in a Paris mag.

Les Points, a bilingual journal, the cover
       glossy yellow,
    in all the kiosks, and good

bourgeois ladies bought it like cheese,
       counting on a knitting
    gazette. The editor,

un grand blond Juif de Hollande, trembla
cinq ans de guerre
caché dans une sombre cave.

Mon ami Citroën eut un succès fou
et bref, et il y a
cinquante ans je suis devenu

en France un écrivain. Les vagues coulent sous
le Pont Neuf
et mes amantes sous les nuages

d'une mémoire qui me chauffe, qui me décime.
Merci, lectrice.
Sois moi. La mort a ses projets.

Elle insiste sur un rendez-vous silencieux
qui me fait peur.
Mon pauvre cœur est un hibou.

a big blond Dutch Jew, trembled
               five war years
      concealed in a dark basement.

My friend Citroën had a wild and brief
               success, and fifty
      years ago I became

a writer in France. The waves flow below
               the Pont Neuf
      and my lovers below the clouds

of a memory that heats and decimates me.
               Thank you, woman reader.
      Be me. Death has her plans.

She insists on a silent rendezvous
               that scares me.
      My poor heart is an owl.

La mémoire est mon bateau

La mémoire est mon bateau
sur la mer un ciel d'eau berçante
les nuages verts sous la mer
là où mes amantes se moquent
de moi comment je suis toujours
une cloche sonnant les vieux jours
un roc conspirant sur Mars
Nous ne sommes que mémoire
J'adore la mémoire dans mon lit.
Sans elle on est roc sur la lune
Ses voix me hantent
sous la mer J'attends sans bonheur
la nuit de silence du port.
Que mon bateau aille où
la mémoire devait être de nouveau
dans le lit avec des voix en mer
C'est vrai que j'étais sauvage
mais serai-je plus tendre
quand elles et moi ne sont que mer?

Memory Is My Ship

Memory is my ship
I like the sea sky of rocking water
the green clouds under the sea
there where my lovers gossip
about how I am always
a bell sounding the old days
a rock conniving on Mars
Memory is all we are
I love memory in my bed
Without her we're rock on the moon
The voices haunt me
below the sea I wait joyless
for the silent night of the port
for my ship to go where
memory was to be again
in bed with voices now at sea
It's true I was wild
but will I be gentler
when they and I are only sea?

Lumière noire

L'encre est une lumière noire.
Je n'ai pas d'âme, mais cette encre
trace la mer sous mes paupières,
et sous la mer un ciel d'esprit
joue dans le théâtre de peur
où de temps en temps je peux voir
(une illusion bien entendu)
le cosmos avec les yeux ouverts.

Black Light

Ink is a black light. I've no soul
but this ink draws the sea
below my eyelids, and below
the sea a sky of mind
plays in the theater of fear
where from time to time I see
(an illusion of course)
the cosmos with open eyes.

Train d'automne

J'écoute la gorge du train,
cri de l'automne qui commence,
cri du blé dans mon lit de vin.
Le train transporte les souvenirs,
le train cargo bleu de la nuit.
Mon père et moi voulons sortir
de chez les morts. La nuit de pluie.
Pris par la pluie nous regardons
les voitures qui courent et qui
nous menacent. Voilà, mon frère!
Tous se lèvent des suicidés,
mes deux frères et puis mon père.
Le train nous ressuscite tous.
Écoute. Pas trop loin. Il traîne
les souvenirs de l'automne doux.

Autumn Train

I hear the throat of the train,
cry of autumn now beginning,
cry of wheat in my bed of wine.
The train transports memories,
the train blue cargo night ship.
My father and I want to leave
the place of the dead. Night of rain.
Trapped on the street in rain we look
at menacing cars. They feign
threats upon us. Look, my brother!
They all arise from suicides,
my two brothers and my father.
The train resurrects us all.
Listen. Not too far. It pulls
memories of a gentle fall.

Sur la blanche ile de peur

où notre maison se noie sous la pierre
et le sang de famille sous la mer,
un corbeau à midi mâche la lumière.
Je n'embrasse qu'un horizon de fer

où le soleil et la lune s'endorment
déprimés. J'oublie qui je suis,
et le chant d'oliviers inscrit le tort
de la chute de ma fille tombe. J'entends son cri

d'un ciel d'ondes sur la mer noire de nuages.
Les becs de trois mouettes déchirent
le courage. En admirant le sauvage
elle devient un olivier et sa troupe.

Debout sur la blanche île de peur je note
qu'on ne peut voir qu'avec le cœur.
Sois calme, tu réclamais le soir, on flotte,
nous tombons, heureux oubliant la peur.

On the White Island of Fear

where our white house, drowning under stone
and family blood, drops under sea,
a midday crow chews light into bone.
I hug only the horizon's iron quay

where sun and moon sleep together
depressed. I forget who I am, and why
the chant of olive trees inscribes
the wrong of my daughter's fall. I hear her cry

from a sky of waves on a sea of clouds.
The greedy beaks of three seagulls snap
her courage. In admiration of the wild
she becomes an olive tree and its troupe.

Standing on our hill on the white island of fear
I know one sees only with the heart.
Be calm, you asked for evening, it swerves,
we are falling and seem happy, forgetting fear.

La vie des poètes

Life of the Poets

Sauvez-moi, docteur

Mouillé et rêvant dans la tranchée,
sa tête un déluge de tableaux
de fusées blanches et balles sombres pour
les cartes d'amour à Lou,
poète gravement blessé au crâne,
fiers de ses bandages

comme dans le croquis de Picasso,
Guillaume passa
une semaine dans une cellule sinistre
de la Santé, accusé
d'avoir volé la Joconde. Mensonge.
Ce n'était pas Guillaume

mais il souffrit priant: «*Prends en pitié
mes yeux sans larmes et ma
pâleur.*» Quand après-guerre il rentre à Paris,
un peu paralysé,
il s'évanouit souvent, mais la folie
le bénit. Il invente

le mot surréalisme et assemble
Calligrammes, épouse
la jolie rousse. Grand Apollinaire.
La grippe asiatique
l'affaiblit en l'an trente-huitième
de sa vie, l'an affreux

des poètes. Le prince dans son lit
vite se dépérit.
La peste est dans le sang, «*Sauvez-moi,
docteur. Épargnez-moi.
J'ai tellement en moi que je veux dire.*»
Et le Pont Neuf se rompt.

Save Me, Doctor

Soaked and dreaming in the trench, his head
a flood of pictures
of white flares and somber bullets for
love letters to Lou,
poet gravely wounded in the skull,
proud of his bandages

as in the sketch by Picasso,
Guillaume once spent
some days in a sinister jail cell
of La Santé, accused
of stealing the Mona Lisa. Unfair
it was not Guillaume

but he suffered, beseeching: *Have mercy
on my tearless eyes and my
pallor.* After the war when back in Paris,
a little paralyzed,
he faints often but the same madness
blesses him. He invents

the word surrealist and puts *Calligrammes*
together, marries
the pretty Russian. Grand Apollinaire.
The Asian flu
finds him weak in the thirty-eighth year
of life, the terrible year

for the poets. The prince in his bed
quickly loses color.
The plague is in his blood. *Save me,
doctor, spare me.
I have so much in me I want to say.*
And the Pont Neuf breaks.

Graves rayons

Poudre tragique tonne dans sa tranchée

le clown du cœur Apollinaire

joue avec nous en portant un collier

de shrapnel et de soleil sa lumière

Grave Rays

Tragic powder booms in his trench

Apollinaire clown of the heart

plays with us wearing a necklace

of shrapnel and sun for his light.

Jours de Paris, 1942

Penser que si je suis arrêtée ce soir (ce que j'envisage depuis longtemps), je serai dans huit jours en Haute-Silésie, peut-être morte, que toute ma vie s'éteindra brusquement, avec tout l'infini que je sens en moi.

Hélène Berr, *Journal* (1942-1944)

La Juive en sortant du métro
avec son étoile mal cousue
est saisie. Sombre Gestapo.
Les mecs de menottes la saluent.
L'étoile jaune sur sa poitrine
est sa lune d'antiquité.
Le Juif inventa la vitrine
pour trop de dieux d'éternité.

La Gestapo créa le coup
de grâce pour ceux qui le matin
ne peuvent plus être debout.
La mort les boit comme le vin.
Le Juif inventa la vitrine
pour trop de dieux d'éternité.
L'étoile jaune sur leurs poitrines
est leur soleil d'antiquité.

Days of Paris, 1942

> To think that if I am arrested this evening (which I've envi-
> sioned for a long time), I will be in Haute-Silésie in eight days,
> maybe dead, that my whole life will be suddenly extinguished
> with all the infinite I feel in me.
>
> Hélène Berr, *Journal* (1942-1944)

The Jew coming up from the métro
with her star too loosely sewn on
is arrested. Black Gestapo
whose handcuffs greet her with a frown.
The yellow star worn on her breast
is her moon of antiquity.
The Jew invented glass cabinets
for too many gods of eternity.

The Gestapo created the coup
de grâce for those who with the dawn
can't make it to their feet. They shoot.
Death swallows them like wine.
The Jew invented glass cabinets
for too many gods of eternity.
The yellow star worn on their chests
is their sun of antiquity.

Max Jacob le jour où il a été saisi
par la Gestapo, le 24 février 1944,
au monastère de St. Benoît-sur-Loire

Picasso peignait toute la nuit. Tu dormais
et quand l'Espagnol tomba dans le lit à l'aube
dans la petite chambre meublée, tu sautas
sur la chaise pour écrire tes poésies et bâillas.
Un lit pour les deux artistes. Tu étais pauvre
toujours. Puis tu vis la lumière et mis ton âme
chez les moines. Tu jouais toujours le fou
et décrivais des bouchers avec jumelles
dansant dans les rues du Japon lointain
où la lune avait des puces. Tes livres brillaient
dans les librairies de Paris, les caves de Max.
Un après-midi la Gestapo te découvrit.
Tes moines frères essayèrent de te sauver.
J'ai ta peau! tu blaguas en te moquant des puces
qui t'avaient mordu, et courageusement
tu jouas avec les mots jusqu' à la fosse.

Max Jacob the Day He Was Seized

                    by the Gestapo, February 24, 1944,
                    at the St. Benoît-sur-Loire Monastery

Picasso painted all night long. You slept
and when the Spaniard took the bed at dawn
in the small furnished room you shared, you leapt
back to the chair to scribble poems and yawn.
One bed and two young artists. You were poor
always. Then you saw light and moved your soul
in with the monks. You always played the fool
and wrote of butchers with binoculars,
dancing the streets of far Japan whose moon
had fleas. Your books shone in the librairies
of Paris—Max's caves. One afternoon
the Gestapo found you. Your monks tried to save
you. *J'ai ta peau!* you joked, mocking the lice
that bit you, bravely punning to the grave[5].

---

[5] *J'ai ta peau* means "I've got your flesh." The French phrase is cruel and also mimics
the word Gestapo pronounced in French.

Chanson d'amour de Robert Desnos
pour Youki

Oui, je suis raréfié comme le fil de fer qu'on lie
au contour des nuages d'hiver
et fiévreux comme la chaleur sous les champignons
quand la forêt autour d'un village normand
fume avec un naufrage sous les paupières des sangliers.
à Tereisienstadt je suis toujours à trois jours de la mort.

Je reste en vie parce que je rêve de toi férocement.
Je rêve de toi à travers les ombres de baïonnettes de carbone,
à travers les collines de dents d'or volées et cette plate-forme de bois
où nos amis sont pendus notoirement
en public uniquement pour nous.
Et quoique mon typhus ne m'épargne que ces heures
pour t'envoyer un message par une étudiante polonaise,
Je rêve encore de toi comme si mon cerveau était fait
des bras d'acier merveilleux
qui te tiennent et qui sont tenus par toi.

Réfléchis, une fois je t'avais dit, tu étais un troupeau de bœufs
éloigné de moi, t'arrêtant indifférente, insouciante,
et tu ne pouvais pas m'aimer,
même si je marchais à travers mes passions hors du monde
vers mes passions les plus herculéennes
et je devenais un érudit d'amour, un pédant aux yeux de diamant,
mettant ma folie au bas de la page autour d'une table d'étoiles.
Mais alors je ne t'avais pas, tu ne m'avais pas, et je ne t'avais pas quittée
comme ce camp sinistre nous a créés disparus,
ou ainsi pensaient les maîtres.
Je suis trop épuisé maintenant de la fièvre du camp pour être
quelque part sauf avec toi.

Love Song of Robert Desnos
for Youki

Yes, I am rarefied like wires that tie sunflowers
around the winter clouds
and feverish like the heat under mushrooms
when the forest around a Normandy village
is smoking with a shipwreck below the eyelids of wild boar,
and still three days away from death in Teresienstadt.

I stay alive because I dream you fiercely,
I dream you through the shade of carbon bayonets,
through hills of stolen gold teeth and that wooden platform
from which our friends are hanged notoriously
in public, just for us.
And though my typhus spares me only these hours
to send you a message through a Polish student,
I go on dreaming you as if my brain were made of marvelous
steel arms that hold you and are held by you.

Think, I once said you were a herd of oxen
remote from me, stopping indifferent,
and you couldn't love me
even if I stepped through my passions out of the world
into my most Herculean passions
and became a scholar of love, a diamond-eyed pedant
footnoting my madness around a table of stars.
But then I hadn't had you, nor you me, and I hadn't had you gone,
as this evil camp has made us gone—
or so the masters thought.
And I am too weary now from camp fever to be anywhere
but with you.

J'ai rêvé de toi dans les matinées quand le soleil oubliait
qu'il était une fleur
avec un devoir de nous nourrir de sa beauté distante et impérissable.
J'ai rêvé de toi au crépuscule
quand les avions tombaient comme le sucre dans le café, dispensant
l'espoir aux enchaînés,
et ce soir je rêve de toi puisque je t'aime
et même mon sang qui est réticent à danser par le sentier de soie
sur ses chevaux de bois adolescents
(je suis fauché et pas un franc à y verser),
mon sang encore siffle pour toi. Tu m'entends
Je t'entends furieusement et je t'aime sereinement dans la nuit.
Le soleil est faible et trop lent pour s'arranger
avec les rossignols et l'aurore
pour venir vite ici lumineux avec ta figure,
pour emporter tes yeux, ta gorge, à ce camp maintenant libre,
et arriver à moi à l'heure dans mon ombre brûlante.

I have dreamt you in the mornings when the sun forgot
it was a flower
with a duty to feed us its aloof and imperishable beauty.
I have dreamt you at dusk
when airplanes dropped like sugar into coffee, spreading hope
to the shackled.
And tonight I dream you, since I love you,
and even my blood, which is reluctant to dance on the silk path
on its amazing adolescent carousel
(for I have run out of francs to slip into it),
my blood still whistles to you. Do you hear me?
I hear you fiercely and love you serenely in the night.
The sun is weak and too slow to conspire
with nightingales and dawn
to hurry here bright with your face,
to carry your eyes, your throat to this now free camp
and reach me in time in my burning shade.

---

[6] Robert Desnos (1900-45), a leading French surrealist poet and friend of Picasso, Artaud, Breton, Hemingway, and Dos Passos, he was active in the Resistance movement. After his arrest he wrote a love poem to his wife Youki. He died of typhoid in the Germaan death camp at Teresín a few weeks after its liberation. His poems written in the camps were later destroyed by accident.

Arthur Rimbaud

À quinze ans tu délirais loin
par les soirs bleus d'été, intime

du blé, pissant vers les cieux bruns
très loin, haut, les poches crevées,

la tête baignée par l'air frais,
heureux comme avec une femme.

Plus tard tu vas à Paris mais
à la gare tu rates Paul

et arrives seul chez lui et poses
tes bottes crottées sur le couvre-

lit qui était blanc et maintenant brun.
Ce drap de mariage est la ruine

de Madame Verlaine. Toi
tu te couches avec le mari faible,

poignardes un poète parnassien
dans la main. En te réveillant

tu embrasses l'aube. C'est midi.
Tu vois un minaret au fond

d'un puits, des cathédrales dans un
lac et des anges sur les pâtures

d'émeraude et acier. Tu es
l'enfant mystique. Tu es Dieu.

Arthur Rimbaud

When you are fifteen you wander far
on blue summer evenings, intimate

with wheat, peeing toward the brown skies
far and very high, your pockets torn,

your naked neck bathed in fresh air
of dusk, happy as if with a woman.

Later you go to Paris but miss Paul
at the station and foot it alone

to his house, plank your muddy boots
on Madame Verlaine's bedspread

which once was white and now is muck.
This sheet of marriage is the ruin

of Madame Verlaine. You sleep
with her weak husband, stab

the hand of a Parnassian poet
reading at a banquet. On waking

you kiss the dawn. It is noon.
You see a minaret at the bottom

of a well, cathedrals in a lake
and angels over pastures

of emerald and steel. You are
a child mystic. You are God.

*

Verlaine te charme et dégoûte
grâce à sa lâcheté humaine

mais tu écris les évangiles.
L'inconnu exige de l'invention:

le nouveau. Après une saison
en enfer—l'époux infernal

toi et la vierge hystérique—
après ta faim d'escalader

et pleurer dans la brume verte,
les noisetiers, et inventer

les voyelles, attendre le temps
de l'amour saisi quand tu dînes

sur les rocs, le charbon, le fer,
l'air—ô bonheur ô saisons ô

châteaux! Mais après la tendresse
de l'éternité impossible,

du soleil mêlés à la mer,
tu cesses d'être Dieu, mesures

ton dégoût par une volée
de jeunes visions. Au revoir

vieille Europe. Bonjour Afrique.
Un homme physique au soleil.

*

Verlaine charms and revolts you
with his cowardly weaknesses,

but you write scriptures.
The unknown demands inventions:

the new. After a season
in hell—you the infernal groom

after with the foolish virgin—
your hunger to climb the tower

and weep in the green mist
and hazels and invent

vowels and wait for the time
when love seizes, and dine

on rocks, coal, iron, the air—
O happiness O seasons O

castles! After the tenderness
of impossible eternity

of the sea mixed with the sun,
you cease being God, measure

your disgust with flight
from young visions. Goodbye

old Europe. Good morning Africa.
A physical man in the sun.

*

Personne ne te voit après
ta disparition de Chypre.

En bateau tu navigues le Nil
et donc tu as de la haute fièvre,

inactivité syphilitique.
Au Zimbabwe une jeune fille

de la tribu Harari vit
avec toi pendant une année.

Tu la soignes, et presque heureux
il te faut de l'argent. Le Roi

Menelek de Shoa t'escroque
trafiquant en armes. Peut-être

tu gagnes de l'argent au marché
aux esclaves. Tu crois en la science

et en ton compagnon serviteur
Djami. Ce serait un plaisir

d'apprendre le piano et peut-être
avoir un fils assez instruit

pour être ingénieur. La botanique
de l'Éthiopie mérite des articles

dans les journaux savants. Ici
à Harar tu vis de la mauvaise

No one sees you again after
you disappear from Cyprus.

By boat you sail down the Red Sea
and then run a high fever,

syphilis and inactivity.
In Zimbabwe a young woman

from the Harari tribe
lives with you for a year.

You care for her, and almost happy
you need money. The King

Menelek of Shoa fleeces you
in gun running, though maybe

you get some money out of
slave trading. You believe in science

and your companion servant
Djami. It would be good

to learn the piano, perhaps
have a son fully educated to be

an engineer. The botany
of Ethiopia deserves articles

in learned journals. Here
in Harar you live with rotten

nourriture entre des indigènes
pourris, pas de poste, pas de

route, trois âmes sur un chameau.
Le climat est bon, la tumeur dangereuse.

Après des souffrances atroces,
tu loues une caravane pour

te porter dans une civière
jusqu'à Aden, le roc horrible,

*

«Ma très chère sœur Isabelle,
à Marseille ils ont amputé

ma jambe. Je suis complète-
ment paralysé, malheureux,

et désemparé comme un chien.
J'aimerais rentrer à la maison

pour un temps, à Roche
où il fait frais, mais demain je meurs.

Je te prie d'envoyer trois mille
francs à Djami. Pour toi, ma chère,

mon dernier transport:
défenses d'éléphant et saphirs.»

food among corrupt natives.
No mail, no highway,

three souls on a camel.
The climate is good but the tumor

dangerous. After atrocious pain
you hire a caravan to

carry you on a stretcher
to Aden, the horrible rock.

*

"My dear sister Isabelle,
in Marseilles they cut off

my leg. I am completely
paralyzed, unhappy,

and helpless like a dog.
I would like to go home

for a while to Roche
where it's cool, but tomorrow I die.

Please send three thousand francs
to Djami. For you, my love,

I have assigned my last shipment
of uncut sapphires and tusks."

L'après-midi avec Tristan, 1949

Le soleil rôdant dans le Flore se pose dans tes yeux un pourquoi?
Tu as trop vu, dans le le cri de vapeur sang
d'un homme doux, des souvenirs

de la Résistance. La mort te chassa dans les cigarettes,
dans les ruelles, la géographie de la peur, et tu souris,
tirant tes livres

de ta serviette pour montrer à ce jeune homme sur une chaise,
lisant tes livres oubliés. *«Mais moi comme poète
on m'ignore. Je suis l'histoire,*

c'est tout.» Sami Rosenstock, Juif de la Résistance, l'inventeur
du Dada, éventail de flammes sur le volcan,
qui connaît le métro de la tombe,

le muscle du violine des caves, la larme non formée formant
un cœur complexe de crachat extrêmement triste,
tu souffres de joie. Ce n'est pas

ta faute. Mon frère manqué, Tzara,
tes livres sur la table du café c'est toi,
la lettre du cabaliste triste.

Tes gros échecs soutiennent ma vie.

An Afternoon with Tristan, 1949

Sun prowling in the Café Flore poses in your eyes of why?
You've seen too much, the cry of vapor in the blood
of a sweet man, of memories

of the Resistance. Death hunted you in a cigarette case,
in the alleys, in the geography of fear, and you smile,
pulling your books

out of your briefcase to show this young man in the chair,
who reads your forgotten books. *"But as a poet they don't
know me. I am history,*

nothing more." Sami Rosenstock, a Jew of the Resistance,
inventor of Dada, fan of flames on the volcano, who knows
the subway of the tomb,

the muscle of a violin of caves, the tear unformed forming
a complex heart of extremely pitiful spit,
you suffer from joy. It's not

your fault. My missing brother, Tzara,
your books on the table of the café are you,
the letter of the sad Cabalist.

Your fat failures hold up my life.

Dansant grec avec Jean-Louis Kérouac, 1959

Je n'attendais pas du tout Jack. J'avais dîné
avec Gregory Corso dans une cave bleue
à New Haven. C'était lui qui devait arriver
       pour lire sa poésie

à Wesleyan. En parlant de Jack, Corso sombra
dans la nostalgie. Je protestai, «Kérouac
n'est pas mort. Il vit, écrit. Qu'est-ce que tu racontes? »
       Corso, le plus straight

de la bande, me confia savoir, «Ginsberg dort
avec tout le monde. C'est une pute, Allen,
mais je suis le seul mec qui ait couché avec Jack.
       Nous sommes tight.»

Corso a raison d'être fier de son copain,
Jack, qui a un rendez-vous sombre avec le whisky,
la maladie bruyante. Une fois dégrisé,
       Le voilà timide.

Le week-end, Greg arrive. Il est accompagné
d'un clochard, qui porte un imperméable noir
et crasseux, un feutre noir, et des lunettes
       de soleil noires.

On dit que c'est Kerouac. «Jamais de la vie!»
j'entends. Ivre, les jambes en coton, il sourit
beaucoup. Puis je l'emmène à la bibliothèque
       où je le présente

au professeur Greene, expert en chants de Noël.
Jack lui demande, «Qu'est-ce que vous enseignez,
monsieur?» «Shakespeare,» répond la grande figure
       patricienne. «Vous aimez

Dancing Greek with Jean-Louis Kérouac, 1959

I was not expecting Jack. I had eaten
with Gregory Corso in a blue dive
in New Haven. He was supposed to show
    to read his poems

at Wesleyan. Talking about Jack, Corso fell
into nostalgia. I objected, "Kerouac's not dead,"
He's alive, writing. What are you talking about?"
    Corso, the straight pin

of the gang, let me know, "Ginsberg sleeps
with everyone. Allen's a whore,
but I'm the only guy who's slept with Jack.
    We're tight."

Corso is right to be proud of his pal,
Jack, who has a dark rendezvous with whisky,
the noisy sickness, though once dried out
    he is timid.

On the weekend, Greg shows. He's come with
a tired bum wearing a black and filthy
raincoat, a black fedora, and black
    sunglasses . . .

"Hey, that's Kerouac." "You gotta be kidding!"
I hear. Drunk, his feet made of cotton,
he's smiling a lot. Then I take him to the library
    and introduce him

to Professor Greene, whose field is Christmas carols.
Jack asks him, "What are you teaching,
sir?" "Shakespeare," responds the patrician
    figure. "Do you like

Shakespeare?» énonce Jack. «J'adore Shakespeare,»
réplique le professeur. Joyeux, Jack s'exclame,
«Moi aussi j'adore Shakespeare!» Et il prend
        la tête de son ami

et peint un baiser énergique sur ses lèvres.
«J'ai lu tous vos livres,» dit Greene. «Je les aime.
Je vous emmène quelque part?» Et les deux érudits
        s'en vont ensemble.

                *

Le soir, la lecture. Corso m'étonne. «Est-ce qu'on
va se faire battre?» «Tu es fou,» est ma réponse,
mais il ni lit pas ses poèmes. Il parle un peu
        sur son héros William

Burroughs, et lit un chapitre de *Naked Lunch*.
Nous sommes transportés dans la jungle, les piqûres
d'héroïne que Burroughs fait dans le cul
        d'un garçon brésilien.

Après le discours sur l'amour, Gregory, Jack
et un tas d'amis de New York, nous allons tous
à une petite chambre. Jack est sobre et il détaille
        la montée à l'aube

du Mont Tamalpais, près du Golden Gate Bridge.
«J'ai grimpé Tamalpais,» Jack dit passionné.
«J'ai vu le point du jour. Je l'ai vu, satori!»
        «Tu as vu bullshit!»

insiste Corso. «J'ai vu de la merde,» avoue
Kerouac. Il n'y avait rien à faire. Jack se rend.
Un de mes amis, qui savait que j'aimais tout
        ce qui est grec,

Shakespeare?" enounces Jack. "I love Shakespeare,"
replies the professor. Overjoyed, Jack shouts
"I love Shakespeare too!" And he grabs
        his new friend's head

and paints an energetic kiss right on his lips.
"I've read all your books," said Greene. "I'm love 'em.
Can I take you someplace?" And the two scholars
        leave together.

                    *

Evening, the reading. Corso stuns me. "Are they
going to beat us up?" "You're mad," I tell him,
but he doesn't read his poems. He says a bit
        about his hero William

Burroughs, and reads a chapter from *Naked Lunch*.
We are transported to the jungle, the shots
of heroin that Burroughs sticks in the ass
        of a Brazilian boy.

After the discourse on love, Gregory, Jack and
a bunch of friends up from New York, we all go
to a small room. Jack is sober and describes
        his dawn climb

up Mont Tamalpais, north of the Golden Gate.
"I climbed Tamalpais," Jack says, impassioned.
"I got to the top and saw daybreak. I saw satori!"
        "You saw bullshit!

Corso throws in. "I saw bullshit," Jack confesses.
There was nothing else to do. He surrenders.
One of my friends, who knew I was crazy about
        everything Greek,

passa un disque. Un kalamatianos des îles.
«Dansons,» Jack me dit, et il me prend par le bras
et nous dansons très bas, presque sur les genoux,
jusqu'à l'aurore Zen.

puts on a record, and island kalamatianos.
"Let's dance," Jack tells me. We squat, arms locked,
and are dancing very low, almost on our knees,
        until Zen daybreak.

Les SDF[7]

Pascal avait son abysse à l'intérieure, et Baudelaire
marche dans les rues du crépuscule avec ses clochards
par un Paris ténébreux tandis que les affamés regardent
la Seine vide. Les ivrognes luttent contre le froid,
et une mendiante avec son pot de feu
souffle dans les brindilles brûlantes pour chauffer
leurs mains et leurs tétines tombantes. Le pire c'est l'aube
quand les Hôtels de Dieu étendent un bras
pour attirer les mourantes vers un lit catholique d'espoir.
Tant que Pascal flâne sur les flammes et blessures
de l'enfer et Baudelaire en décadence
a pitié des damnés comme lui, les morts sans-abris
sentent mauvais dans les portes de New York. Pourtant,
quand la brume s'éteint, les âmes tombent goutte à goutte
de leurs corps et elles s'échappent en innocence.

[7] Sans domicile fixe.

Homeless

Pascal has his abyss inside, and Baudelaire
walks in the twilight streets with the clochards
through dingy Paris while the hungry stare
across the empty Seine; dull drunkards spar
with cold, and beggar women with a can
of fire blow on the burning sticks to warm
their hands and sagging breasts. Worst is the dawn
when the Hotels of God extend an arm
to draw the dying to a Catholic bed
of hope. While Pascal tramps the sores and blaze
of hell and Baudelaire in decadence
pities the damned like him, the homeless dead
smell bad in New York doorways. Yet when haze
burns off, their souls leak out in innocence.

Chansons de métro

Quand je vois un enfant dans le métro d'Athènes,
recueillant des drachmes pour sa mère qui chante
en serbe ou albanais des mélodies perçantes,
je pense à un garçon dans le métro de Boston,
vendant des journaux. Mon père, à douze ans,
SDF, avait quitté la maison, l'école,
et sa famille. Il couchait dans je ne sais quels coins
de la ville. Il survivait. Me voici. Et il mangeait
au bars des ouvriers. Ces hommes l'aimaient bien,
il dit. Il chantait aussi. Pas dans le métro
mais tout seul dans sa chambre chez nous. Puis il partit.
Je prenais les trains pour le voir à Mexico,
au Colorado et puis ces villes n'étaient plus,
mais je l'entends chantant dans les wagons d'Athènes.

Subway Songs

When I see a child in the Athens metro,
collecting drachmas for his mother singing
piercing melodies in Serbian or Albanian,
I think of a boy in the Boston subways,
selling newspapers. My father, then twelve
and homeless, had left school, home and family.
He was sleeping in I don't know what corners
of the city. He survived. Here I am. And he ate
in workers' bars. These men liked him a lot,
he said. He also sang. Not underground
but at home all alone in his room. Then left.
I took the trains to see him in Mexico,
in Colorado and then the cities were no more
but I hear him singing in the Athens metro.

Poètes dans la lune

Le soleil sans mots lance la lumière
qui éclaire l'air suave et la chaleur
pour Ève et Adam. Puis tremblant de peur
ils jouissent en fabriquant nos pères
et meurent. Mais les poètes qu'on aime
dans la lune, je les entends sous l'arche
d'un obscur brouillard sauvage où ils sèment
mon âme avec la douce nuit qui marche.

L'orphelin de Antoine de Saint-Exupéry

Petit prince, tu as beaucoup voyagé
jusqu'aux astéroïdes, pris ton déjeuner
avec un ivrogne et un astrologue
assis sur le ciel haut comme une drogue.
Pilote de guerre, ce fou d'éclair,
ton père de fer écrit sous la mer.

Poets in the Moon

The wordless sun launches a light
flaring out with delicious air and heat
for Eve and Adam. Shivering with fright,
they have fun creating our ancestry,
and die. Yet those poets whom I feed
on in the moon, I hear below the arch
of a somberly wild fog where they seed
my soul with a gentle night on its march.

The Orphaned Prince of Antoine de Saint-Exupéry

You, little prince, you've voyaged right
up to asteroids, shared a bite
with an astrologer and a drunk
seated on the sky high on junk.
A downed war pilot of mad clarity,
your iron dad writes below the sea.

Lettre à l'inconnu

J'écris un mot à l'inconnu.
À quoi bon? Je n'ai rien à dire
sauf que sauve-moi. Tu m'as vu
dans le cru miroir. C'est pour rire,
je suis loin de l'esprit français
et triste. Alors je prends un vol
de nuit avec saumons plus frais
que l'idée barbare de vol-
er par le ciel pour boire un peu
de rosé dans une cabane
bleue dans le Midi moins le quart.
Tu m'attends. Je suis nerveux,
fou de délire et toi, l'arcanne
sagesse et les bras de beaux arts.

Letter to an Unknown

I scrawl a note to an unknown.
What good is it? I've nothing to say
but save me. You saw me, my frown
in the raw mirror. I laugh away,
remote from any French mystique
and sad. So I take a night flight
with salmon—fresher than the bleak
barbaric whim of a flying freak
through the sky—to drink a light
rosé deep in a blue cottage on a lane
buried almost in Provence. You
wait for me. I a nervous mad heart
over you and you an arcane
wisdom, the arms of the fine arts.

Bérgère des étoiles

La tour Eiffel marche sur les rues
de Paris dans la brume d'hiver.
Ses lumières te font flotter nue
au ciel de blé, courant dans l'air.
La tour Eiffel marche sur les rues.

La ville dort, ne brûle pas,
l'artiste se lève. Dans le cerveau,
le soleil anime les pauvres et toi
tu erres par la nuit, par la pluie sans peau.
La ville dort, ne brûle pas.

Danse sur la pâture des étoiles.
La tour Eiffel, l'ange poids lourd
d'acier, remplit ses bars demi-mals
de tartes aux framboises et rendez-vous.
Danse sur la pâture des étoiles.

La pâture sera froide ou chaude
et toi l'acrobate rimbaldienne
d'un rêve cosmique, d'un saut
à la demi-lune, gamine radieuse.
La pâture sera froide ou chaude.

La tour Eiffel marche sur les rues
de Paris par ses bars demi-mals
et dans la brume flotte nue
où elle est bérgère des étoiles.
La tour Eiffel marche sur les rues.

Shepherd of the Stars

The Eiffel Tower walks the streets
of Paris in a winter fog.
Her light floats you nude to sky wheat
and grass. Above the air you jog.
The Eiffel Tower walks the streets.

The city sleeps and doesn't burn,
the artist wakes. Sun in her brain
and in the poor gives heart to turn
and walk through night and fleshless rain.
The city sleeps and doesn't burn.

Dance on the pasture of the stars.
The Eiffel Tower, the heavyweight
steel angel, stocks demimonde bars
with framboise tarts for her sky date.
Dance on the pasture of the stars.

The pasture will be cold or hot
and you a Rimbaud acrobat
out of a cosmic dream have shot
to the half moon, your beaming brat.
The pasture will be cold or hot.

The Eiffel Tower walks the streets
of Paris by her demimonde bars,
in fog floats you up nude to wheat
where it is pastor of the stars.
The Eiffel Tower walks the streets.

Chambres des Orphelins

Rooms of the Orphans

Chambre du fils du joaillier

Mon père était joaillier
et j'aime faire des colliers
de lapis et de perles d'eau fraîche
qui me portent aux montres
dans le style de Le Corbusier,
que mon père dessinait
sous le nom de Pierre Grange,

les jours de mon enfance,
et ces montres étaient en acier
et en verre comme les gratte-ciels,
mais plus beaux étant austères
comme les kouroi archaïques,
et minces comme une adolescente
qui s'allonge sur ta peau.

Les colliers d'argent et perles
je les donne avec une bague
ou un bracelet à des amies
qui souvent en sont heureuses.
Quant à la bague, selon
l'habitude de mon père
je ne connais pas le sentiment

intime d'en avoir porté.
Mes doigts sont crus et nus,
et cette pratique de l'absence
ne blesse personne.
Pourtant je sens une intense
mélancolie. Ça peut expliquer
pourquoi certains jours de l'année

Room of the Jeweler's Son

My father was a jeweler
and I like to make necklaces
from lapis and fresh water pearls
that send me back to watches
in the style of Le Corbusier
that my father designed
under the name of Pierre Grange

in the years of my childhood,
and those watches were of steel
and glass like skyscrapers,
but more beautiful being austere
like archaic kouroi
and thin like an adolescent girl
who is lying down on your skin.

The necklaces of silver and pearls
I give along with a ring
or bracelet to friends who
often are happy with them.
As for the ring, in keeping
with my father's practice,
I don't know the intimate

feeling of having worn one.
My fingers are naked and raw,
and this practice of absence
wounds no one,
yet I feel an intense
melancholy. That may explain why
some days of the year

je sors mes gobelets d'argent,
les seules dépouilles mortelles
de mon père déprimé après
le bond de l'ange à l'ombre,
son saut du haut d'un gratte-ciel,
et je bois un peu de vin
dans l'argent de Pierre Grange.

I take out my silver goblets,
the only mortal remains
of my depressed father after
his leap from a skyscraper,
the swan dive to shadow,
and I drink a drop of wine
in the silver of Pierre Grange.

Chambre des orphelins, 1947

Après le suicide de mon père, Marti,
ma belle-mère mexicaine,
revint au lit de fer avec sa mère
Rebeca, une séfarde de Constantinople,
qui couramment m'appelait mancebico,
le jeune homme en espagnol médiéval,
mais elle avait peur que je prenne
sa fille comme mon père l'avait fait.
Ils louaient des chambres derrière
la grande cathédrale, un petit taudis
dans le vieux quartier. Moi aussi
je vivais cette année à Mexico,
tout près dans un orphelinat.

Si je n'étais pas rentré avant dix heures
(je donnais des classes partout
dans la ville pour gagner des pesos)
j'étais obligé de passer
les nuits à lire dans un café, ou mieux,
j'allais chez Marti et dormais
sur une natte de paille sur le plancher
entre la petite bonne indienne
et son frère Sam, capitaine de l'armée.

Souvent lorsque j'étais fauché,
je vendais mon sang dans une clinique,
un samedi deux fois, mais pas
au même endroit. Bien que l'infirmière
reconnut les piqûres fraîches
elle me laissa passer. La belle Marti
avait deux ans de plus que moi.

Room of the Orphans, 1947

After my father's suicide, Marti,
my Mexican stepmother,
went back to the iron bed with her mother
Rebeca, a Sephardi from Constantinople,
who normally called me mancebico,
young man in medieval Spanish,
but she was afraid I'd get
her daughter as my father had.
They rented some rooms behind
the great cathedral, a small hovel
in the old district. I too
lived that year in Mexico City,
near her in an orphanage.

If I couldn't make it back by ten
(I gave evening classes
all over the city to earn some pesos)
I did an allnighter,
reading in a lowdown café, or better,
went to Marti's and slept
on the straw mat on the floor
between the tiny Indian maid
and her brother Sam, an army captain.

Often when I was broke
I sold my blood in a clinic, and on
one Saturday twice—but not
in the same place. Though the nurse
noticed the fresh pricks
she let me through. Beautiful Marti
was only two years older than I was.

Je l'aimais beaucoup et je ne savais pas
alors que la vente de mon sang
était pour elle un stigmate
que Dieu ne pardonnerait pas.
Pour ma part, quel bonheur de me coucher
chez elle, sur le plancher! D'ailleurs
j'étais ravi de gagner mon pain en donnant
des leçons et du sang au peuple.

I cared for her a lot and never knew
that the selling of my blood
was for her a stigma
that God would not forgive.
For my part, what fun it was to flop
at her place, on the mat! Besides,
I was tickled to earn my bread
giving classes and blood to the people.

Chambre de mon sang inconnu

Morris, un pauvre tailleur à Boston,
habitait la rue de Lait.
Il n'était pas né dans la rue des Rosiers
mais dans le ghetto d'un village
hors de Vilna, mais l'endroit n'est plus,
les nazis l'ayant aplati avec
leurs chars d'assaut. Comme lui, il est absent
de l'histoire visuelle.
Il faisait son métier modestement,
et après la mort de deux femmes
(la première à la naissance de mon père)
il finit ses jours
avec une noire de Boston, sa femme
dans un appartement humble.

À douze ans mon père quitta l'école
et sa maison, puis vendit
des journaux dans le métro. Tant de rage
il garda contre le tailleur
que je n'ai jamais pu le voir. J'ai tant
de nostalgie. Je songe
à l'inconnu, mon grand-papa Morris,
et une nuit dans son salon
où nous bavardons jusqu'à l'aube, parlons
de sa fuite de la Pologne,
de nos secrets, et d'un costume très chic
qu'il a déjà cousu pour moi,
que je porte toujours en descendant
l'escalier de son atelier.

Room of My Unknown Blood

Morris, a poor tailor in Boston,
lived on Milk Street.
He wasn't born on the rue des Rosiers
but in a village ghetto
outside Vilna, yet the place is no longer,
the Nazis having flattened it
with their tanks and, like him, it is missing
from visual history.
He performed his trade modestly
and after the death of two wives
(the first one at my father's birth)
he ended his days
with a black woman from Boston, his lady
in a humble apartment.

At twelve my father left school
and his house, and sold
newspapers in the subways. So much rage
he kept against the tailor
that I never could see him. I've so much
nostalgia. I dream
of the unknown, my grandpa Morris,
and one night in his living room
we gossip until dawn, speaking
about his flight from Poland,
about our secrets, and a very chic suit
he's already sewn for me
that I am still wearing as I descend
the stairway of his shop.

Chambre d'un génie

Mon nom est Howard Barnstone. Je suis né
comme mon frère Willis
dans une ville du Maine, haut dans le nord
où la neige, une adolescente
de l'hiver, apparaît timidement,
trop jeune dans l'année.

Ici c'est la vieille France. Les gens
comme Jack Kerouac
sont pour la plupart Québécois, avec l'air blanc
du bouleau, la céramique bleue
dans les grands yeux et parfois dans l'esprit.
Nous luttons sur la glace

pendant les froids après-midi, fous
de hockey. Rien de plus
jusqu'à la guerre et l'on m'envoie comme officier
de la marine à Marseille. Le pied!
Je deviens ami avec Raf. Plus tard
nous fabriquons un livre

sur la ville d'Annie de Galveston,
Bresson fait les photos,
moi le texte. On dit que je suis snob. Et c'est vrai,
mais je fais mon possible pour
sauver les amis et les inconnus.
Mieux si on pouvait me sauver.

J'en ai besoin. J'ai un certain succès
d'estime. Un architecte
risqué, sauvage, glorieux. Avec Mark, le peintre,
qui est même plus désespéré
que moi, nous faisons la Chapelle Rothko
et les grands tableaux noirs

Room of a Genius

My name is Howard Barnstone. I was born
                                        like my brother Billy
in a city in Maine, up in the north
                            where the snow, an adolescent
of winter, appears timidly,
                                    too young for the year.

Here it is old France. The people
                            like Jack Kerouac
are for the most part Québécois, with a white air
                            of the birch, the blue ceramic
in their large eyes and sometimes in the mind.
                    We fight on the ice

during the freezing afternoons, hockey
                            maniacs. Nothing else
until the war and they send me as a naval
                    officer to Marseille. A blast!
I become a friend of Raf. Later
                    we two do a book

on the city of Annie of Galveston,
                            Bresson takes the pictures,
I do the text. They say I'm a snob. It's true,
                    but I do all I can to
save friends and strangers. It would be better
                    if one saves me.

I need it. I have a certain success
                            of prestige. An architect
daring, wild, glorious. With Mark, the painter,
                    who is even more despairing
than me, we do the Rothko Chapel
                            and the great black paintings

c'est lui. Je partage le bleu sur noir,
une beauté qui exige
la vie. Avec Billy je parle peu. Nous sommes
d'un lait commun, c'est clair qu'on s'aime.
La tristesse s'impose. Qui comprend
la chute dans le noir

qui me fait causer d'une voix si faible
qu'on ne peut pas m'entendre?
Faisant mon métier je construis des bâtiments
composés d'éléments de la terre.
Je me pousse. Je suis le fou
joyeux. Je m'empoisonne.

La cachette des pilules allemandes
accomplit sa mission.
J'avais gribouillé un mot: «*Je vous aime tous.*»
C'est vrai, je vous ai tous aimés,
mais pas moi-même. Affreusement
triste, je me rejette.

is he. I share the blue on black,
                a beauty that demands
your life. With Billy I speak rarely. We are
                of common milk, it's clear we love.
        Sadness imposes. Who understands
                the fall into the black

        that makes me talk in a voice so weak
                one can't hear me?
Doing my job I construct buildings
                concocted of elements of earth.
        I push myself. I am the happy
                madman. I take poison.

        The cache of German pills
                accomplishes its mission.
I had scribbled a word: *I love you all.*
                It's true, I've loved all of you,
        but not me. Horrifyingly
                sad, I reject myself.

Chambre du somnambule

Mes amis me taquinent me disant
distrait, dans la lune. Ils ont raison
mais ils ont tort car je suis somnambule,
        je ne dors pas

la nuit, et pendant le jour le corps glisse,
une pensée dans l'air, automatique
comme tout, un rêve absurde. De qui?
        Je cherche dans

l'ombre qui est moi, tombant dans le néant.
C'est normal. Il y a longtemps que je sais
que je suis somnambule, nuage blanc
        sans centre. C'est

l'horreur habituelle. Je me débrouille
et je suis même heureux quand je m'oublie
avec toi qui ne me demandes rien
        de fantastique

sauf de t'aimer. Je suis incapable
de m'aimer, de trouver un sanctuaire
dans le noir où peut loger la bête esprit,
        mais je te vois,

cela suffit. Je suis fatigué d'être
le somnambule. Il t'adore ce monstre,
il songe, écrit et passe pour un homme—
        peut-être la nuit.

Room of the Sleepwalker

My friends tease me calling me
absent-minded, lost on the moon. They're right
but they're wrong since I'm a sleepwalker,
           I don't sleep

at night. During the day my body slides,
a thought in the air, automatic
like everything, an absurd dream. Of what?
           I look in

the shadow that is me, falling into the zero.
It's normal. I've known for a long time
I am a sleepwalker, a blank cloud
           with no center.

It's the usual horror. I manage
and I am even happy when I forget
with you who ask me nothing
           of the fantastic

except that I love you. I am incapable
of loving me, of ascertaining a sanctuary
in the black where the dumb spirit dwells,
           but I see you.

That's enough. I am weary of being
the sleepwalker. Yet this monster adores you.
He dreams, writes and passes for a man—
           maybe the night.

La chambre

Ma chambre c'est moi dans laquelle mon corps
garde un peu de lumière.
Ce n'est pas aussi sombre que je te dis.
Un fantôme je suis
mais toi aussi, bien que tu aies de la chance
d'être sauvée de l'eau
noire dans les veines. Viens. La chambre vide
a besoin de ta pluie
trompe-l'œil. Un, deux, nous serons trempés.
La chambre de l'oubli.
Dans la chambre d'extase, de sang,
tu sors tes lèvres de Paris.

The Room

My room is me in which my body
holds a bit of light.
No, it's not as dark as I tell you.
I am a phantom
but you too, though you could be lucky
and saved from dark
water in your veins. Come. The empty room
needs your trompe-l'oeil
rain. One two and we are drenched.
The room of forgetting.
In the room of ecstasy, of blood,
you bring out your Paris lips.

Chambre d'un Carmélite

Enterre-nous dans une
girouette, dans un mot indicible.
Je suis un moine
Carmélite, Juan,
et dans une nuit obscure je sors

inaperçu, ma maison étant
en paix. En secret et déguisé, dans l'ombre
je descends l'escalier
dans l'ombre et ne vois
personne. Dans cette nuit joyeuse,

je ne vois nulle chose,
ni guide ni lumière quelconque sauf
le soleil dans mon cœur.
Alors l'ombre
me guide plus sûr que la clarté

du midi où elle attend,
où il semble que personne n'ést.
L'amant avec l'amante,
l'amante dans l'amant
transformée. En plein oubli endormis.

Puis perdus parmi les lis
sous la chambre du ciel, deux ventres devient
une lune, je veux
dire nous deux
tournant dans une blanche girouette.

Room of the Carmelite

Bury us inside
a weathervane, in an unsayable word.
I'm Juan, a Spanish
Carmelite monk,
who in a dark night go out

undetected, my house
at peace. In secret and disguised, in darkness
I go down the stairway
in darkness and no one
sees me. And in this joyful night

I see no thing at all,
no guide or light at all save for
the sun in my heart.
Then darkness
guides me more certain than the glaring

noon, where she waits
where it seems that no one is.
Lover with the beloved,
beloved in the lover
transformed. In oblivion we sleep.

Lost among the lilies
under the room of the sky, two bellies
become a moon,
meaning we two
spinning in a white weathervane.

Chambre près du jardin

Quand je mourrai j'aurai de graves problèmes.
Le jour sera un corbeau, l'ombre me tentera.

Elle m'embrassera avec des étincelles de princesse
allumant la chute. Quelle tromperie!

La sainte merde! Quelle vache barbare
la petite politicienne

pour qui je ne suis qu'un zéro sur la feuille du calcul
du passé. En respirant

Je me libère de la nausée. Plus fort que la mort
est le paradis de nous dans ta chambre près

du jardin (la mort est furibonde), où nous tombons
ensemble dans les draps bleus infinis.

Room by the Garden

When I die I will have grave problems.
The day will be a crow, darkness lure me,

hug me with her sparks of a princess
lighting the plunge. What duplicity.

Holy shit! What a barbaric
mendacious cow, the tiny politician

for whom I'm zero on the spreadsheet
of the past. Breathing I'm free

from nausea. Stronger than death
is paradise of us in your garden

room (death goes bonkers) where we fall
together into blue infinite bedsheets.

Chambre de rêve

Si je plonge au lit tard je dors, mais je m'agite

toute la nuit et suis incapable de tomber des

sommets au sonnets, de nager dans le lac gris

en moi. Je me lève crevé, m'habille vite

et me rends heureux à la page, et quand l'éclair

me frappe je joue aux voyelles, attendant l'aube.

 Sommeil? J'en ai assez pris dans ma vie. Dans

la queue de la boucherie j'attends, en gribouillant

(mon vice voluptueux), je délire, bouffon d'espoir.

Puis ma petite-fille et moi nous montons sur

les chevaux de bois. La chambre de rêve tourne partout.

Room of Dream

If I flop on the bed late I sleep, but I toss

all night and am incapable of falling from

summits into sonnets, of swimming into the gray lake

inside, I get up wiped out, slip on a robe

and surrender happy to the page, and when lightning

hits me I play with vowels, waiting for dawn.

Sleep? I've had my share of it in my life. In

a line at the butcher shop I wait, scribbling

(my voluptuous vice), a delirious buffoon of hope.

Then I climb onto wooden horses with my

granddaughter. The room of dream spins everywhere.

Chambre d'amour

La paix après la jouissance, le lait d'Éden
dans la chair bien au fond des belles côtes
qui sont les murs de l'amoureuse dans ce soleil
intérieur qui est notre village. Rien que nous
deux pauvres types déposés dans ce monde.
Pour deux jours nous abolissons les continents.

Room of Love

Peace after climax, the milk of Eden,
the room in the flesh below the lovely ribs
that are walls of the lover in this sun
inside, which is our village. Nothing but
we two poor types dumped in this world.
For two days we abolish continents.

Chambre de Paris

Ouvre la fenêtre et laisse entrer l'air nocturne
avec sa mémoire parfaite des rues.
Dans la rue Jacob les fenêtres des caves

étaient de petites librairies avec seulement
des titres couleur rubis sur les livres crème
des maîtres français. Comme des bijoux

ils luisaient sous la vitrine. Gide et le mot juste
de Flaubert. À minuit les tomes étaient
toujours illuminés. Un magasin avait un poème

d'Henri Michaux, signé par l'auteur à l'instant
où il prenait des drogues expérimentales.
1948. L'eau chaude dans ma chambre.

J'aimais une œuvre condamnée, *Les fleurs
du mal*, un cadeau d'une jeune juive, tachée
de rousseurs, que j'aurais dû poursuivre.

Ces emblèmes de la perfection, propres
comme les alexandrins de Racine étaient
bizarres pour un étudiant cru, fanatique,

bon et jamais accompli selon le critère
de ses propres yeux. Je n'ai pas paniqué.
Devant moi j'avais une vie. Peut-être j'irai faire

de la peinture aux Beaux Arts, resterai en Europe
et choquerai la princesse royale anglaise, hurlant à poil!
quand elle visitera mon atelier. Peut-être je finirai

Paris Room

Open the window and let the nocturnal air come in
with its perfect memory of the streets.
On the rue Jacob the windows of the basements

were some bookstores with only
ruby-colored titles on cream-white books
by the French masters. Like jewels

they glistened under the store window. Gide
and Flaubert's right word. At midnight the tomes
were always lighted. A store had a poem

of Henri Michaux, signed by the author
at the instant he was on experimental drugs.
1948. There is hot water in my room.

I liked the condemned work, *Flowers
of Evil*, a gift from a young freckled Jew
whom I should have gone after.

These emblems of perfection, correct
like Racine's alexandrine meters,
were weird for a crude student fanatic,

good and never accomplished at the level
of his own eyes. I didn't go haywire.
Before me I had a life. Maybe I'll paint

at the Beaux Arts and stay in Europe
and shock the royal English princess, screaming
Strip! when she visits my studio. Maybe I'll end up

dans un bordel espagnol en y cherchant une leçon
de chair. Il se peut que je grimpe dans mon lit
avec mes livres rares des caves et que les laisse

chauffer mes draps, ou que je trimballe mes papiers
autour de la Méditerranée dans une malle
de matelot jusqu'à Tanger, et les fasse imprimer

sur velum, en fontes de rubis, et les regarde trembler.
Ces pages doivent me donner l'élan de traîner
sur cette planète d'imperfections. Rien de cela.

Dans une pagaille totale, acrimonieusement,
une page sans merci me regarde fixement et méprise
mes framboises desséchées et mes doigts arthritiques.

in a Spanish whorehouse looking for a lesson
in flesh. It may be that I'll climb into bed
with my rare books from the basements and let them

heat my sheets, or I'll cart my papers
around the Mediterranean in a sailor's trunk
all the way to Tangier, and print them

there on vellum in ruby fonts and watch them shiver.
These pages should give me the spunk to drag
around this planet of imperfections. Nothing

comes close. In this huge clutter, acrimoniously,
a merciless page glares at me, disdaining my bag
of dried up raspberries and my arthritic fingers.

Chambre de rendez-vous dans l'inconnu

C'est arrangé. Nous trouvons une ville ou un cottage
à l'étranger et nous passons la nuit à raconter
　　　les jours jusqu'à l'aube

et un bruit soudain ou le cauchemar du doute
nous réveille et nous partons, toi à tes os et la poussière,
　　　et moi au lavabo pour me laver

la gueule et affronter le blanc d'absence.
Je t'aimais et je t'aime tellement que tout paraît naturel
　　　et infini. C'est facile

quand je rêve, mais j'avoue que souvent je me demande
pourquoi tu m'as laissé seul? Je suis fautif, oui,
　　　je le sais. J'aurais dû venir

tout de suite à New York. Tu m'as appelé et j'ai vacillé.
Puis c'était tard et tu as sauté du bâtiment.
　　　il n'y avait que la fuite

sans retour. Nous retournons constamment à nous.
Ton fils te garde et tant que je vivrai, tu vis un peu,
　　　trop rare mais assez

pour me faire frissonner. Ces rares jours tu es le vent
de jadis. Je te sent près. Alors nous marchons toujours
　　　dans le vent. En sommeil,

en oubli. Le pire c'est les yeux ouverts et je souffre
de joie. Je ne dois pas me plaindre. Le miracle
　　　dure. Je suis avec toi.

Rendezvous Room in the Unknown

It's arranged. We find a city or a cottage abroad
and we spend the night gossiping about
      the days until dawn

and sudden noise or the nightmare of doubt
wakes us and we leave, you to your bones and dust,
      I to the sink to wash

my mug and confront the blank of absence.
I loved you and love you so much it all seems natural
      and infinite. It's easy

when I dream, but I admit often I wonder why
you left me alone? I am at fault, yes, I know it.
      I should have come

immediately to New York. You called and I wavered.
Then it was late and you jumped from the building.
      There was nothing left but flight

with no return. We come back constantly to each other.
Your son keeps you. As long as I live, you live a bit,
      too seldom but enough

to make me shiver. Those rare days you are the wind
of the past. I feel you near. Then we walk, always
      in the wind. In sleep,

in oblivion. The worst is with open eyes and I suffer
from joy. I shouldn't complain. The miracle
      lasts. I am with you.

Chambre de la science profonde

La pensée exige la grammaire
mais la raison n'est que des mots
nourrissant un bruyant cerveau.
Sous le cerveau gît le mystère
dans un sensuel jardin de rêve.
Vas-y et jouies la science d'Eve.

Chambre du voyage

Le matin je grimpe la neige
de ce village jusqu'aux monts de pin
qui me gèlent ici à Québec.
Le lait dans le ciel veut tousser,
il me fait peur mais je le bois,
et triste je me lève et marche
de mon lit à l'Afghanistan.
Puis, quand les Taliban dorment
parmi les framboises de sang,
les femmes brûlant leurs burlas
ont l'étoile de l'aube dans les yeux.

Room of the Deep Science

Thought needs a grammar tree
yet reason offers only words
feeding a brain of noisy birds.
Below the brain lies mystery,
garden dream where naked you leave
for rapture and the science of Eve.

Room of the Voyage

In the morning I climb the village
snow to the pine mountains
that freeze me here in Québec.
The milk in the sky wants to cough,
which scares me but I drink it,
and in sorrow I get up and walk
from my bed to Afghanistan.
There, while the Taliban dream
amid the raspberries of blood,
the women burning their burqas
keep the star of daybreak in their eyes.

Chant nocturne des Enfants Invisibles

Night of the Invisible Children

Chant nocturne des enfants invisibles

Dans la forêt d'Ennuyeuse Tristesse
j'ai perdu le ruisseau de mon chemin.
Le soleil noir me voit errant sans cesse.
Son feu en moi sert à aveugler ma fin.

J'attends dans la forêt de Longue Attente
la lune de lys et d'orfèvrerie
qui habille les arbres non existants
et nous égarés sous le vent des cris.

Dans la forêt des enfants échappés
du camp d'extermination, tous se cachent
craintifs dans l'Hôtellerie de Pensée;
tous sont tués par des cerveaux de hache.

J'attends dans la forêt de Longue Attente
petits enfants du monde—les malades
gazés—tournant jolis, tournant présents,
chevaux de bois brûlés dans leur gambade.

Teresienstadt, 2003

174

Night Song of Invisible Children

In the forest of the Bothering Sadness
I lost the brook that was my bubbling road.
The black sun sees me roaming borderless.
Its fire in me are cries blinding our end.

I wait in the forest of the Endless Wait
for a moon of lily and filigree
to dress up every non-existing tree.
We are bewildered under Winds of Hate.

In the forest of children who escape
from this city extermination camp,
the others cower in the Inn of Thought
but all are murdered by a pointing hand.

I wait in the forest of the Endless Wait
for children of the world, tiny ones gassed,
spinning in carousel beauty, spinning here,
wooden horses burning in escapade.

Teresienstadt, 2003

Nuit des dictionnaires

J'habite les dictionnaires. Mes chambres.
Je suis parmi eux jusqu'à la nuit blanche
      quand les mots m'abandonneront
et ce corps sera un néant sans paroles,
      nu et tranquille.

Souvent je m'écroule et tombe en noyant
dans le ciel d'encre des lettres nageantes,
      viles pédantes qui me taquinent,
puisque ces orgueilleuses me connaissent,
      un mendiant devant

leur bouches, qui sont aussi creuses que
ma langue morte, qui ne sont pas plus profondes
      que l'eau de la couleur
d'encre sèche dans les grandioses tombes
      muettes sans moi.

Je proteste parce que je bois les entrées,
l'alcool noir, moi toxicomane, ravi
      parmi elles. Mais
j'arrive à leur page, étranger, quémandant
      un mot pour en finir.

J'écris. Rien à faire. Je fais mon possible
dans une langue que j'adore et connais mal.
      À l'intérieur vit le noir.
Je veux finir tôt et passer enfin sans mots
      dans le silence.

Night of the Dictionaries

I inhabit dictionaries. My rooms.
I am among them until the white night
      when words abandon me
and this body will be a wordless nothing,
      naked and calm.

Often I collapse and fall drowning
in the sky of ink of swimming letters,
      vile pedants who tease me
since these pompous gents know me,
      a beggar before

their mouths that are hollow like
my dead tongue, who are no deeper
      than the water of the color
of dry ink in the grandiose mute
      tombs without me.

I protest because I drink entries,
black alcohol, I an addict, exalted
      among them.
But I reach their page, a foreigner,
      begging a word to end.

I write. Can't help it. I do my best
in a tongue that I love and know poorly.
      Inside lives the black.
I wish to finish soon and pass wordless at last
      into silence.

Nuit de tes yeux

Je suis le mystérieux, le parvenu,
et vis goutte à goutte et meurs d'une goutte
de poison du temps qui ne reviendra plus.
Mon vent est foutu. Aveugle sur la route

des néants dans son abîme de morts
noircis, sans souci je n'ai plus de vœux,
et habitant l'absence, mon nid tes yeux
loin dans l'extase d'être lu, je dors.

Night of Your Eyes

I am the mystery man, the nouveau riche,
and live drop by drop and die on a drop
of time's poison, illusions now on a leash.
My wind is blown. Blindly strolling the loop

of those nonbeings in their abyss of black deaths,
carefree with my longing lost for keeps.
Rooming in absence from your eyes, a nest
remote with the ecstasy of being read, I sleep.

Nuit de la chute

Sur le pont je reçois un bon mot de la nuit
      et ne me penche pas sur le parapet.
      Le fleuve est habillé de brume et de lys,

ce qui est normal en été. Je ne tombe pas
      dans l'eau. Sous l'eau il n'y a que le soleil
      ombrageux dans les yeux d'un corps sombrant,

mais une mince jeune femme habillée
      de chagrin cherche la lumière de la paix,
      pour apaiser et tromper l'esprit un peu.

Elle décide de plonger dans le vide.
      Je la vois tomber et il est déjà tard.
      J'arrête ma motocyclette. Puis,

me repentant d'une irrésolution, je pense
      aux mots méchants dont elle a dû souffrir,
      je la rejoins, et nous buvons la paix ensemble.

Night of the Plunge

On the bridge I receive a good word of the night
        and don't lean over the parapet.
        The river is dressed in fog and lily

which is normal in summer. I won't crash down
        on the water. Under the water is only shady
        sun in the eyes of a sinking corpse,

but a skinny young woman who is dressed
        in sorrow is looking for the light of peace
        to appease and fool the spirit a bit,

and she decides to plunge to the bottom of emptiness.
        I see her falling and it's already late.
        I stop my motorcycle. Then,

repenting of my irresolution, I think about
        the nasty words she must have endured,
        join her, and we drink peace together.

Nuit d'un exquis matin aztèque

J'avais une chambre étroite sur le toit
de notre pension pauvre à Mexico.
Écris-moi si tu vis. J'ai honte. C'est toi
qui m'as mis sur la terre. Ton nom est fragile.
Je t'avais connue vaguement à l'école
et tu recommandas cette maison. J'y suis.
À la table nous mangeons souvent ensemble.

Les soirs je lis dans ma cellule blanche.
À dix-neuf ans mes cuisses jettent la chaleur
comme l'ampoule seule au-dessus de mon lit.
À l'aube je vois Popo[8] qui fume lentement
comme le patron du kiosque en bas,
vendeur des oranges qui cachent au centre
une lune verte de chaudes plaines de Vera Cruz.

J'entends un floc d'eau pleuvinant juste
contre la fenêtre. La bonne indienne
prend une douche. Sa nudité fait rougir
le prince Popo. Elle est de mon âge. Vite
elle s'habille et part. Je suis allongé
sur le dos, les yeux tranquilles, et la porte
s'ouvre. Quelqu'un d'autre grimpe par

l'échelle au toit. C'est toi. Tu laisses tomber
ta jupe, lèves le drap et t'allonges sur moi.
Tu manges ma bouche et t'assois
sur l'arbre qui ne connaît pas la pluie
au centre de l'orange. Je monte au soleil.
Nous sommes lumière. Puis tu te lèves et quittes
l'air. Si tu vis je suis là sur le drap.

[8] Popo est le volcan Popocatepetl, en Azteque «mont fumante.»

182

Night of an Exquisite Aztec Morning

I had a narrow room on the roof
of our poor pension in Mexico City.
Write me if you're alive. I'm ashamed. It's you
who put me on the earth. Your name is fragile.
I knew you vaguely at the school
and you suggested this house. I'm there.
At the table we often eat together.

In the evenings I read in my white cell.
At nineteen my thighs shoot out heat
like the lonesome bulb above my bed.
At dawn I see Popo[9] who is smoking slowly
like the owner of the kiosk at the corner,
seller of oranges that hide in their center
a moon green with hot plains of Vera Cruz.

I hear a plash of water drizzling just
outside the window. The Indian maid
is taking a shower. Her nakedness makes
prince Popo blush. She is my age. Quickly
she dresses and leaves. I'm stretched out
on my back, eyes tranquil, and the door
opens. Someone else has climbed up

the ladder to the roof. It's you. You let
your skirt drop, lift the sheet and lie on me.
You eat my mouth and sit down on
the tree that doesn't know the rain
in the center of the orange. I rise to the sun.
We are the light. But you get up and dress
and go. If you're alive I'm here on the sheet.

[9] Popo is the volcano Popocateptl, in Aztec "smoking mountain."

Nuit du suicide

Je ne veux pas quitter de l'atmosphère,
flottant sur l'aile noire du suicide.
Jeune j'aimais à la folie mon père
qui en voyant son échec choisit le vide,
un gratte-ciel d'où il sauta dans l'air
de mai pour que le bruit des cris stupides
se terminent, le laissent dormir. Mon frère,
l'auteur d'une architecture limpide
dans une grange austère de bois gris,
vit son échec et mâcha du poison
et nous laissa coupables comme lui
qui était gelé par le silence con.
Frère ou père, j'ai peur de moi ce soir.
Dis dans mon lit que je vis dans le noir.

Night of Suicide

I do not want to leave the atmosphere,
floating on the black wings of suicide.
I loved my father. In my eighteenth year
he saw his failure and he chose the void,
leaping from a skyscraper into the air
of May so that the noise of stupid screams
would end and let him sleep. Then my brother,
the author of an architecture clean
as in his austere barn of weathered oak,
saw his failure. He swallowed poison pills
and left us all guilty like him. He broke
from snowing pain to lie down dumbly still.
I'm scared of me. Brother or father, give
me light. Say in my bed of night I live.

Nuit d'un con

J'ai peur. Je suis con. Je ne suis pas vieux
mais ma vie est une mélancolie en panne.
Bien que je me fasse passer pour heureux,
mes enfants m'appellent hooligan

car je ne dors pas. Je fais mon boulot,
même dans le lit où je suis ravi
car je compose. Ils disent que bientôt,
sans faire ce que je veux je suis fini.

Mes amantes sont les gros livres et elles
me consolent. Mon travail de cochon
ne se révèle point en elles qui sont belle-
ment proprettes, réglées sur leurs rayons,

de bonnes tranches de porc chez le boucher
qu'aime un pédant. Et je t'aime beaucoup,
toi sur mes genoux. Je ne t'embrasserai jamais
bien que je sois assis rêvant de toi, ce fou

croyant qu'il est bon de toucher ta peau.
Tu vois? À cinq heures, pas endormi.
D'un délire et d'une joie lâche en mots,
avec l'espoir de la nuit, je t'écris.

Night of the Idiot

I'm scared. I'm an idiot. I'm not old
but my life is a melancholy broken down.
Though I force myself to seem cheerful,
my children call me a hooligan

since I don't sleep. I get through my work,
even in bed where I am in delirium
since I'm dreaming up stuff. They say soon
without doing what I want I'm done for.

My lovers are heavy books and they
console me. My piggish labors don't even
hint that those fat books, beautifully
proper and orderly on the shelves,

are good slices of pork at the butcher,
which a pedant loves. And I love you a lot,
you on my knees. I never embrace you
though I sit delusional dreaming you,

believing it's good to touch your skin.
You see? It's five a.m. and not asleep.
From delirium and cowardly joy in words,
with hope in the night, I write to you.

Nuit bête

Quand je suis triste et ça arrive souvent
comme souvent la neige de l'automne
tombe trop tôt, mes projets sont du vent,
ma mélancolie je la partage bonne
avec Guillaume, artiste des fusées
de guerre, et ris, lis, pleure bouche bée.
Dans le désespoir la nuit m'aime un peu
et je suis con de vouloir être heureux.

Dumb Night

When I'm sad and I'm in that bind
often as often autumn snow
falls too soon and projects unwind,
I let my melancholy grow
sharing it sweetly with Guillaume,
artist of war rockets. I moan,
laugh, read, despair, yet night likes me
a bit, a dope to wish to be happy.

Nuit des visiteurs

Je suis rentré chez moi, un visiteur.
Mon père était un visiteur de nuit
et avant le réveil de nos voisins
partit à l'aube par l'escalier de fer
dans l'intestin du bâtiment, la voie
des porteurs de charbon. Enfant, j'étais
avec lui, nous deux vus par le Hudson.
Il m'embrassa. Mais j'ignorais toujours
la prochaine fusion de Mère et Père.
Bientôt le gros poids de la mort fixa
la fin de leur tendresse. Plus de peur.
Je suis mon père, l'étranger chez soi.
Nos maisons ont des ailes fabriquées
pour anges confus. La mélancolie
comme brume du nord a son pouvoir.

Night of the Visitors

I've come back home, a visitor.
My father was a visitor by night
and before our neighbors woke
he left at dawn on an iron stairway
through the building's guts, the path
of the coalmen. A child, I walked out
with him, we two seen by the Hudson.
He kissed me. But I never knew
the next fusion of Mom and Dad.
Soon the gross cargo of death fixed
the end of tenderness. I don't fear.
I am my father, stranger in his home.
Our houses are fabricated wings
for confused angels. Melancholy
like northern fog has its powers.

Vignt cafés du monde et un à l'aube

Twenty Cafés of the World and One at Dawn

Café de Charles Baudelaire et Guillaume Apollinaire

Je balance entre le spleen et la joie,
entre Baudelaire et Apollinaire.
Charles le drogué bleu, Gui le soldat,
mais l'un est l'autre, errant dans la gouttière.
J'erre encore, plus vieux qu'eux qui, avec feu
de la parole, dansent au-dessus
de Paris, des jeunes mecs dans les cieux.
Le pain de la paix qu'ils n'ont pas connu.
Je les aime, mes poètes dans la mort
qui allument la nuage et marche de nuit
pour les solitaires. Fredonnant bas
dans l'abîme des disparus, ils sortent,
s'assoient au Café des Anciens Amis
et me donnent à boire bras à bras.

Café of Charles Baudelaire and Guillaume Apollinaire

Between my spleen and ecstasy I waver
between Baudelaire and Apollinaire,
Charles the blue druggy and Guillaume the soldier,
one is the other, roaming gutter and square.
I am still roaming, older than them. There,
with fire of the word they are strolling on
the clouds of Paris, young punks in the air,
but the good bread of peace they haven't known.
I love them. They're my poets who in death
light candles in night clouds and march of dawn
for solitaries. Humming very low,
unseen in their abyss, they leave their earth,
sit at the Café of Old Friends long gone,
and give me drinks, hug me and won't let go.

Café des Deux Magots

Ni monsieur Camus ni monsieur Kérouac
ne boit son vin rouge aujourd'hui à table,
mais la fumée frisée de nos jeunes lèvres
écrit des contes de merveilles sur les nuages
qui il y a quelques années virent des femmes de la Résistance,
hurlantes, alignées et fusillées devant les portes de cuivre
d'un café voisin dans une allé serpentine de la Rive Gauche
ou des acteurs tournant des films en chambres secrètes.
Ce soir des nuages baleines flottantes sont un cadeau furtif
d'art que la nature peint sur les cieux de Paris
pour les innocents et les souffrants.
Solitaire et trop jeune pour le désespoir cru,
je fume ma pipe, mêlant le tabac avec des âmes de souffle bleu.
Asses ici, une salade de visages et de chapeaux,
des inconnus avec mille contes dans le théâtre du café,
nous sommes survivants de la vieille guerre et d'une jeune paix.

Café des Deux Magots

Neither Monsieur Camus nor Monsieur Kerouac
is drinking his red wine today at the table,
but the curly smoke from our young lips
pens tales of the marvelous on memory clouds
that a few years ago saw Resistance women
howling, lined up and executed by the brass doors
of a nearby café on a winding Left Bank alley
or actors making films in secret rooms.
Now floating whale clouds are a shifty gift
of art that nature paints on Paris heavens
for the innocent and those in grief.
Alone and too young for crude despair,
I smoke my pipe, mixing *tabac* with souls of blue breath.
Sitting here, a salad of faces and hats, of unknowns
with a thousand tales in the theater of the café,
we're survivors of the old war and a young peace.

Café Solitaire

Dans les pays étrangers le café est la chaise
        de ma solitude, la table
d'un livre que je déchiffre difficilement
        comme une glace barbouillée

mais qui garde une transparence où se voit
        le gangster, l'amie, le poète,
une figure solitaire dans un café public.
        Ici à Tanger j'ai des soucis,

un stylo, un carnet et la faim qui me lie
        au garçon. Perché sur l'océan
on perçoit l'infini du sud, les ondes fines
        sous la flamme de l'après-midi.

Ce café a sa nouvelle lune de couteau berbère
        qui me voit depuis tant d'années,
choquée que j'existe toujours. Dans le café
        je prends mon livret et sommeille.

Lonely Café

In foreign countries a café is the chair
　　　of my loneliness, the table
of a book that I decipher difficultly
　　　like a besmirched mirror

holding a transparency that shows
　　　a gangster, a friend, a poet,
someone solitary in a public café.
　　　Here in Tangier I've worries,

a pen and notebook, and hunger tying me
　　　to the waiter. Perched over the ocean
I perceive the infinity of the south, fine waves
　　　under the flame of afternoon.

This café has a Berber-knife new moon
　　　looking at me for years and years,
shocked that I still exist. In the café
　　　I seize my little book and doze.

Café du Poème

Ces jours de décembre je porte un fez arabe

sur la tête pour m'abriter

du soleil noir et de la photographie de l'âme.

Voici mon simple atelier

en ville, un café solitaire pour te toucher,

toi qui es invisible, que

je juge. Pour toi obsessionnellement je travaille

en sachant que tu es loin,

intouchable et je te vois sur la table.

Café of the Poem

These days in December I wear an Arab fez

on my head to shelter me

from the black sun and the soul's photograph.

Here is my common studio

in town, a solitary café to reach you in,

you who are invisible,

whom I add up. For you I work obsessively,

knowing that you are far,

untouchable and that I see you on the table.

Café du Rêve

Si tu demandes pourquoi un vieux con
aime rester au lit

toutes les nuits du monde à composer des vers
quand ces bêtises lui gâchent

la santé, je n'ai rien à dire. C'est moi, j'ai peur,
Hard Knocks Café.

Je veux changer, ne veux pas. Tous mes projets,
toutes les promesses s'évaporent.

Je sors rarement. Je suis moine
sans chapelle

et cette histoire éternelle me fait rire.
J'aime le théâtre.

Le matin bâille et je viens d'embrasser un verre
de jus d'orange

et une brioche qui me font rêver
aux planètes de jasmin

qui tourne et tourne autour d'un soleil orange,
et la paix

du papier blanc attendant
moi et mon encre.

Dream Café

If you ask why an old asshole likes to lie in bed
dreaming up verse

every night of the world when this stunt
plunders his health,

I've nothing to say. That's me, scared.
Hard Knocks Café.

I want to change, I don't want to. All my plans,
all my promises evaporate.

I go outdoors rarely. I'm a monk
without a chapel

and this eternal story makes me laugh.
I relish drama.

Yet in the yawning morning I hug a glass
of orange juice

and a brioche and they permit dream
of a jasmine planet

circling and circling an orange sun
and the calm

of blank white paper waiting
for me and my ink.

Café d'Eau pour Inventer la Poésie

Dans la chapelle de la douche il pleut

sur mon cou. Les cheveux et le cerveau

se chauffent, et on disparaît dans le feu

parfait et doux blessant mon Café d'Eau.

Water Café for Inventing Poetry

In the chapel of the shower it rains

on my neck. My hair and brain get hot, my way

to disappear into the fire perfect

and soft, wounding my Water Café.

Café de la Guerre

Souvent à Buenos Aires pendant la Guerre Sale
        je traduis les sonnets
de Jorge Luis Borges qui a un appartement
        sur la rue Maipú juste
en face. Aveugle il ne voit plus la page
        mais il répète ses propres vers
avec une sonorité du ciel. Il s'exclame,
        ¡qué bueno, qué bueno!,
avec le sourire de Fernandel. D'habitude
        nous marchons au Saint James Café
sur Corrientes pour prendre le petit déjeuner,
        son endroit de *charla*

où les grands miroirs montrent son col blanc,
        la tête et les yeux défigurés
et son complet noir et impeccable.
        Notre commérage est Dante
et Milton ou la guerre, une embuscade
        le jour de Noël qui laissa
200 morts et les hôpitaux se remplirent de jeunes
        blessés. D'autres soirs
je me retire chez moi où je répands
        ses livres et labyrinthes
partout sur le plancher, et moi en extase
        toute la nuit, je cherche

en angoisse une forme en anglais pour ses paroles
        en marbre parlant.
Avant l'aube je sors. Maintenant c'est moi
        l'aveugle. L'heure
avant le point du jour c'est pour les ermites.
        Dans un café ordinaire

War Café

Often in Buenos Aires during the Dirty War
    I am translating sonnets
of Jorge Luis Borges who has an apartment
    on la calle Maipú right
across the street. Blind he no longer sees the page
    but he repeats his own lines
with the sonority of the sky. He exclaims,
    Qué bueno, qué bueno,
in his Fernandel smile. Normally
    we walk to the Saint James Café
on Corrientes to have our breakfast,
    his place for a charla

where the great windows show his white collar,
    his head and disfigured eyes
and his black and impeccable suit.
    Our gossip is Dante
and Milton or the war, an ambush
    on Christmas day that left
200 dead and the hospitals filled with the young
    wounded. Other evenings
I retreat to my rooms where I spread out
    his books and labyrinths
all over the floor; and me in ecstasy
    all night I search

in anguish for an English form for his words
    in speaking marble.
Before dawn I go out. Now it's me
    the blindman. The instant
before daybreak is for hermits.
    In an ordinary step-down café

je sirote mon maté dans un pot bleu.
Dans ce souterrain
après l'aube on n'entend plus les bombes.
Seul le bruit d'un buveur
bâillant. Quand il s'en va, je rentre en moi
dans le brouillard.

I sip my maté in a blue mug.
      Here underground
after dawn the bombs are no longer heard.
      Only the rustle of a drinker
yawning. When he leaves, I go back in me,
      into the fog.

Café Sans Nom en Turkestan Chinois

Dieu n'a pas de nom et c'est son mystère.
Alors, on l'appelle *ha Shem*, le Nom.
Sans nom et sans figure vue par nous,
le même anonymat garde
un morceau du désert de Gobi en Xingjang
et un beau café de chevaux

où il n'y a personne. La Route de la Soie
dort sous l'étoile du soleil,
hors de la ville blanche de Kashgar.
Je dors aussi. Ma fille est perdue
dans le grand marché de perles et de pastèques.
Ce n'est pas grave. Ici des bancs

en bois. Un haut garçon Ouïgour arrive.
Tout est calme, yogourt et bagels.
Le garçon impeccable nous aime, crache
sur les bagels, astiquant leur peau.
Nous sommes flattés. Rien ne se passe. Je me
repose content en solitude.

Vers le crépuscule habillant les cimes
de l'Himalaya, je perçois
une mosquée pas loin, abandonnée,
et j'y vais. Maigre, de la merde
sur le sable, des graffiti partout
sur les murs, le dôme résiste

avec une sainteté humble et le parfum
de sa vieillesse. Ici seule
la méditation dans la fraîcheur obscure.
Il ne se passe rien. Ma fille
me découvre. Elle arrive avec une pastèque
et des perles. Un marché roulant.

No Name Café in Chinese Turkistan

God has no name and that's his mystery.
So they call him *ha Shem*, the Name.
Nameless and without a face seen by us,
the same anonymity is kept by
a piece of the Gobi desert in Xingjian
and a handsome horse café

where there is no one. The Silk Road
sleeps under the star of the sun
outside of the white city of Kashgar.
I also doze. My daughter's lost
in the great market of pearls and watermelons.
It's not grave. Here a few wooden

benches. A tall Uigur waiter shows up.
All is calm, yogurt and bagels.
The impeccable waiter likes us, spits on
the bagels, polishing the skin clean.
We're flattered. Nothing happens.
I relax happy in solitude.

Toward the twilight dressing the peaks
of the Himalayas, I make out
a mosque not far off, abandoned,
and I head for it. Barren, with shit
on the sand, graffiti everywhere
on the walls, the dome endures

with a humble holiness and smell
of her old age. Here only
meditation in the dark freshness.
Nothing happens. My daughter
finds me. She comes with a watermelon
and pearls. A rolling market.

Un jeune couple Ouïgour, plein de vie,
s'assoit sur le banc à côté.
Le garçon, le couple, ma fille et moi,
déjà une belle ville entière
dans ce coin du désert où les chevaux
sans noms à vendre nous observent.

A young Uigur couple, full of life,
sits on the next bench.
The waiter, the couple, my daughter and me
already a beautiful whole city
in this corner of the desert where the nameless
horses for sale observe us.

Café du Monde

L'algèbre de la nuit c'est le calme et la flamme
d'un instant rare qui permet un voyage
à l'île blanche du paradis
        et noire de l'enfer normal
                dans une poche du cerveau.

Quand je peux et quand la lumière est généreuse
je reste là-bas. L'esprit est illusoire.
Il justifie le non-sens de ma vie,
        le vide des soirs
                de travail jusqu'à ce que mes yeux

tombent de ma tête. Puis l'heure de sortir,
l'heure de l'ermite vagabond
et de son café du monde. Je sors
        mais souvent simplement en rêve,
                tableaux de Beijing ou de Buenos Aires.

Les cafés des mauvaises rues de Mexico
sont mes chambres de nuit. J'y dors,
j'y lis avant que l'aube me jette
        sur le trottoir sale
                où les monticules d'enfants,

qui dorment et gèlent dans la rue, se dispersent
pour chercher à se nourrir.
Je n'aime pas trop mon orphelinat
        mais j'y prends
                mon pain, café con leche, et une

tortilla de papa, un bon repas pour les gosses
réfugiés de la guerre civile d'Espagne
qui sont mes camarades, pour moi
        l'invité qui couche sur le toit
                dans une hutte blanche: deux lits,

Café World

The algebra of night is the calm and flame
of a rare instant permitting voyage
to an island white with paradise
       and black with normal hell
            down in a pocket of the brain.

When I can and when the light is generous,
I stay down there. Spirit is illusory
and justifies the inanity of my life,
       the hollow of evenings
           of work till my eyes

tumble from my head. Then time to get out,
time of the vagabond hermit
and his café of the world. I go out
       but often simply to dream
           paintings of Beijing or Buenos Aires.

The cafés on nasty streets of Mexico City
are my night rooms. I sleep there
and read there until dawn tosses me
       onto the trashy sidewalk
           where mounds of children,

sleeping and freezing in the street, break up
and go off looking for food. I'm not wild
about my orphanage
       but there I eat bread, tortilla
           de papa, pan dulce, and down

café con leche, a good meal for the refugee
children of the civil war in Spain,
who are my pals, for this guest
       sleeping on the roof
           in a white hut: two cots,

deux chaises et une table pour Tomás et moi,
deux coquins, copains à la Autónima,
lui en chimie, moi en philo.
      Pour gagner des pesos
            je donne des leçons d'anglais

le soir. L'orphelinat ferme ses portails de fer
à dix heures. Alors, pour passer la nuit
c'est soit sur le plancher de ma belle-mère
      avec la bonne indienne,
            ou dans mon café du monde roulant.

Les bouquins que je lis m'emportent loin,
bien loin, un bohémien dans la nature,
heureux comme avec une femme, ou fainéant
      dans une rue étrangère
            où je suis déjà entièrement.

two chairs and a table for Tomás and me,
two buddies enrolled at the Autónima,
Tomás in chemistry, me in letters.
      To earn some pesos
          I give English lessons

in the evenings. At ten the orphanage slams
its iron gates. Then, to spend the night
it's either at my stepmother's on the floor
      with the Indian maid
          or here in my rolling café.

The books I read all night carry me far,
very far, a bohemian in nature,
happy as if with a woman, or loafing
      on a foreign street
          where already I am entirely.

Café des Ports de Mykonos et de Pirée

Après cinq mois à Mykonos, l'île d'igloos
et d'icebergs de soleil,
le seul étranger, *xenos*, juste après la guerre,
grâce à Andonis, mon patron,
maître de danse, et capitaine de la marine,
je danse rembetika.

Andonis pêche des mois dans les Dodécanèse.
À son retour la fête.
Un peu de résiné, mon maître ami me guide
et ensemble la nuit
est blanche comme les ruelles de minuit. Andonis
Hartopoulos - Antoine Fils

de Papier - prophète de mon sort et prison
heureuse. Quand je pars,
la chapelle de Paraportianí ferme l'œil
de son dôme—la glace
du cosmos—et son blanc de chaux brûle irascible,
et ne veut jamais s'éteindre,

même pas ce soir dans la taverne de Tsitsanis
au Pirée, méprisée
et ignoble car Nikos est le meilleur artiste
du monde de bouzouki.
Je bavarde avec le compositeur. La fumée
mélismatique est l'air

de ses chants. Trois ou quatre heures j'écoute
et regarde stupéfié
les danseurs du port. J'ai une envie abominable
de me lever. Enfin,

Cafés in the Ports of Mykonos and Piraeus

After five months on Mykonos, the igloo island
of sun-made icebergs,
as the only foreigner, *xenos*, just after the war,
thanks to Andonis,
my landlord, master dancer, and sea captain,
I dance rembetika.

Andonis fishes some months in the Dodecanese.
When he's back it's a party.
Some retsina and my maestro leads me.
Together the night is white
like midnight alley walls. Andonis
Hartopoulos - (Antony the Son

of Paper) is prophet of my fate and happy
prison. When I leave,
the Paraportianí chapel closes the eye
of its dome—the ice
of the cosmos—and its whitewash burns irascibly
and won't go out,

not even this evening in Tsitsanis's taverna
in Piraeus, disdained
and lowdown since Nikos is the best bouzouki
artist in the world.
I gossip with the composer in the smoky den
of his melismatic

worker songs. I listen for three or four hours,
stupefied, watching
the port dancers. I have an abominable urge
to get up. When at last

la taverne déserte, des hommes finissant
un hassápiko sérieux,

Nikos dit, «*Ela*, Johnny.» Donc, mes jambes,
pas moi, descendent sans peur
d'une icône, et lentes, agiles consument la fumée,
encerclent le feu invisible
sur le plancher de roc dans le dôme de la blanche chapelle.
Bougies, encens, noirceur.

the taverna is almost empty, some men finishing
a serious hassápiko,

Nikos cries, "*Ela*, Johnny." Then, my legs, not me,
fearlessly descend from an icon,
slow and nimbly, consume the smoke
and circle invisible fire
on the stone floor inside the white chapel dome.
Candles, incense, shadows.

Café du Spleen

Je suis un cimetière abhorré de la lune.
« Spleen » Charles Baudelaire

Même Robert Frost connaît le spleen, mais le jour
où nous mangeons seuls dans le Connecticut il parle
sans cesse comme la neige. Sa voix profonde

chante et rit comme les collines vertes de son Vermont.
Son chagrin il le vit. La peau de son visage
l'écrit les nuits où Dieu est malade, gravement.

Son spleen gelé, ami et son copain d'espérance, le nourrit
les soirs tel le poète inventeur d'une fleur du mal
dont la misère toujours le sauve.

Nous, les clients du café de nuit, notre chapelle d'encre,
buvons le danger. Quand les Zeppelins bombardent Paris
et New York, le gang de Frost et Baudelaire (et Blaise Cendrars,

plus fou qu'un zèbre bleu) grimpent la Tour d'Etoiles,
une fois la plus haute du monde, pour guetter les blessés
de la ville, Robert Frost a sa neige et ses hiboux

à traverser avant le sommeil, les Parisiens ont leur drapeau
noir d'angoisse sur leur crâne incliné et les quais de brume
et leurs bonjours aux cloches dans leurs lits de béton.

Café Spleen

I am a cemetery, abhorred by the moon.
"Spleen," Charles Baudelaire

Robert Frost also knows spleen but the day
in Connecticut we eat alone, he talks incessantly like snow.
His profound voice sings and laughs like Vermont's green hills.

He lives his anguish. His splintered face
writes it on the nights when God is gravely sick.
His frosty spleen, a friend and companion of his hope,

feeds the evenings as did its Paris inventor
of a flower of evil, whose misery always saves him.
We the patrons of the night café, our chapel of ink,

drink danger. When the Zeppelins bomb Paris
and New York, the gang of Frost and Baudelaire
(and Blaise Cendrars crazier than a blue zebra)

climb the star tower, once the tallest in the world,
to spy on the city's wounded, Robert Frost
has his snow and owls to walk through before he sleeps

and Parisians have their black flags of angst
implanted on their skulls, and their quays of fog
and bonjours to bells in their beds of concrete.

Café du Malaise

Où que je sois dans mon ermitage banal ou exotique,
l'instant arrive où je n'en peux plus,
                              mes yeux tombent,
je sors et m'assois dans un café quelconque.

Soulagement. Je ne pense pas. Imprévu,
j'ai une voisine de la table
                              qui désire ma main.
La présence de cette dame chic, en noir,

m'inquiète. Je suis crevé mais cela me gène
qu'elle soit invisible. Viens, mon ami.
                              «Je suis ici et je ne vais
nulle part.» C'est l'heure. «C'est l'heure de me laisser

en paix.» Justement. «Justement pas, je te dis.
Tu me dégoûtes.» Viens tranquillement. Si non,
                              j'ai d'autres moyens.
Je ne cause plus avec la dame aux grands yeux,

et prenant un livre ami de ma serviette
je m'adonne à mon plaisir. La dame indignée fait
                              un dernier effort
de m'anéantir mais j'ai horreur de l'éros

de la belle mort qui se vante d'être l'ange
du notre rendez-vous. Dans ce café agréable
                              de réconfort
j'ai soif, je veux lire et aujourd'hui

il pleuvine. Le cosmos mouillé et bienveillant
assombrit la dame et rouille sa montre fatale.
                              «Madame, madame,
Foutes-moi le camp.» J'aime la pluie sur la table.

Café Malaise

Wherever I am in my banal or exotic hermitage
a second comes when I can't stand it,
                        my eyes fall out,
I go outdoors and sit in any café.

A relief. I am not thinking. Unexpected,
I have a neighbor at the table
                        who wants my hand.
The presence of this chic lady in black

upsets me. I'm drained but it hurts me
that she is unseen. Come, my friend.
                        "I'm here going
nowhere." It is time. "It is time to leave me

in peace." Precisely. "Absolutely not, I tell you.
You disgust me." Come quietly. If not,
                        I have other means.
I say nothing more to the lady of huge eyes,

and picking up a companion book from my bag
I dance cheerfully. The indignant lady makes
                        her last attempt
to annihilate me. I'm horrified by the eros

of lovely death posing as the angel
of our appointment. In this pleasant café
                        of recovery
I'm thirsty, I want to read and today

it's drizzling. The wet cosmos kindly
clouds the dame and rusts her fatal watch.
                        "Lady, lady,
fuck off." I adore the rain on the table.

Café du Bonheur

Beaucoup de monde aspire au Paradis, l'île verte dans les cieux,
ou à l'Apocalypse

et ces murailles de diamant, ou au premier jardin où Adam
le lâche et la belle Ève

de courage et le Père trop père se disputaient,
mais je veux me réveiller

comme un ours en hiver devant un croissant au chocolat
et dans la matinée

ou la nuit m'asseoir dans un café et causer avec le garçon
qui me donne de l'eau fraîche

ou un strudel aux pommes ou la vision de l'amour.
J'ai toujours voulu manger

une tarte au bonheur. Je suis trop vieux pour en goûter? Pense pas.
Le garçon me reproche

d'en avoir peur. J'ai la foi. Et un beau matin ou dans
la chambre d'angoisse,

si j'attends, le ciel tombera, cassant mon cou avec éblouissement.
Je peindrai une miniature

de cinq Turks pêchant dans un bateau à voiles ballonnées
et je goûterai la tarte de la joie.

Happiness Café

A ton of people aspire to Paradise, green island in the skies
or that of Apocalypse

and its walls of diamond or the first garden where Adam
the coward and lovely Eve

of courage and the Father, too much father, argued,
but I need to wake

like a bear in winter to jelly doughnuts or an ant to honey,
and in the morning

or night sit down in a café and chat with the garçon
who might give me

fresh water or an apple strudel or the vision of love.
I've always wanted to eat

a cheerfulness pie. Am I too old to taste it? Don't think so.
The garçon scolds me

for being scared. I have faith. And one good morning,
or in my agony room,

if I wait, heaven will drop, breaking my neck with wonder.
Then I'll draw

a miniature of five Turks fishing in a ballooning sailboat
and taste a tarte of joy.

Café de Dieu

Dans la noirceur je songe à une tasse de bon chocolat
mais l'idée d'un dieu n'a pas eu un parfum agréable depuis

mon enfance. Cependant je traduis la Bible. Je suis ridicule.
Un flambeur jouant avec l'esprit. Sûr au moins

de la brume qui a le nom grandiose de conscience,
je suis habitué au désespoir et essaie de ne pas penser

au dôme du néant. Je le sens Dieu c'est déjà trop.
Donc, rien. J'attends et en attendant dans la solitude

du café, j'invite Dieu à s'asseoir ici à ma table.
Je lui commande déjà un café français. Il peut

être muet, mais il a bon goût et d'une façon galloise
nous pouvons passer des heures invisibles car lui aussi

a des problèmes penibles. Entre nous on peut trouver des mots
de silence pour nous consoler sur les grands mystères.

Café God

In the blackness I daydream of a cup of good chocolate
but the idea of a god hasn't had a pleasant smell since

my childhood. Yet I translate the Bible. I am ridiculous,
a Jack of Spades playing with spirit. Sure at least

of a haze that has the grandiose name of consciousness,
I am used to despair and try not to think of the dome

of nothing. I feel God and that's already too much.
Well, nothing. I wait and while waiting in the loneliness

of the café I invite God to sit down here at the table.
I've already ordered him a French coffee. He may

be mute, but he has good taste, and some Gallic way
we share the long invisible hours since he also

has a few aching problems. Between us we can find words
of silence to console us about the big mysteries.

Café de Prière

Dieu, pourquoi suis-je un malheureux?
La sirène de nuit crie. Les ponts tombent.
La guerre ferme les bouches de l'Afrique
et de l'Asie, mais je ne souffre pas
de leurs misères. Tu n'est pas psychologue.
On n'exige pas que tu me répondes,

mais si tu avais un grain d'existence
ce serait joli. Je pourrais m'éloigner
de l'ennui du lit, la boîte de peau
que je frotte, pour le vol noir inconnu
dans l'infini. Je ne me plains pas
et préfère la misère au vide,

mais ma belle camarade tu es
le néant. Dieu, ferme ta gueule. Tu es gentil
en silence, et à toi je confie la magie,
le sourire d'une montagne chinoise.
Trop près du silence, j'arrive au
salon de tango. L'ermite danse.

Dieu, pourquoi suis-je un malheureux?
La sirène de nuit crie. Les ponts tombent.
Je danse avec toi, bouche sans bras
dans le café de prière rythmique
et vois que tu glisses comme Madonna.
Mon Dieu, je suis heureux cette nuit.

Café Prayer

God, why am I a malcontent?
The siren of night cries. Bridges fall.
War shuts the mouths of Africa
and Asia, but I am not suffering
from their miseries. You are not a shrink.
No one asks you to answer me,

but if you had a wink of existence
it would be glorious. I could depart
from bed ennui, from a box of skin
I scratch, to an unknown black flight
into the infinite. I'm not beefing
and prefer my misery to a void,

yet my beautiful companion, you are
a gorge. God, close your mouth. You're nicer
silent, and I confide magic in you
as in the smile of a Chinese mountain.
Too close to silence, I take off for
a tango hall. The hermit dances.

God, why am I a malcontent?
The siren of the night cries. Bridges fall.
I dance with you, armless mouth
in the café of rhythmic prayer
and see you slide and dip like Madonna.
My God, I am happy tonight.

Café des Champs

Peut-être qu'il existe une chambre dans le ciel,
blasonnée avec des gadgets du Paradis
et des jouets blancs pour les aventuriers de l'âme
qui sautent libres dans le brouillard invisible

ou sous la terre un énorme trou de couleurs
pour la peau qui a besoin de brûler en extase
contre la peau et oublier les confins terrestres,
mais je connais des champs et des forêts d'hiver

et ce jour je marche dans la froideur avec
ma petite fille Zoé, qui symbolise la vie.
J'ai une radio dans la paume de la main
et des bois nous débouchons sur un pré gelé.

Sur un étang de glace et de neige nous dansons
la valse de Chopin qui échappe de ma main.
Ma Zoé a presque cinq ans et moi j'en ai six
et nous dansons et dansons à l'infini chaude.

Café of the Fields

Perhaps there exists a room in the sky,
blazoned with the gadgets of Paradise
and white toys for adventurers of the soul,
who leap freely in the invisible mist

or under the earth an enormous hole of colors
for flesh that needs to burn in ecstasy
against flesh and forget terrestrial confines,
but I know some fields and winter forests

and today I'm strolling in the cold with
my granddaughter Zoe, who means life.
I have a radio in the palm of my hand
and from the woods we come on a frozen meadow.

On a pond of ice and snow we are dancing
the Chopin waltz that escapes from my hand.
My Zoe is almost five and I am about six
and we dance and dance into hot infinity.

Café Zéro avec le Docteur Franz Kafka

À Prague je dîne avec le docteur Franz Kafka,
        le Houdini de la parole,
chez lui, sur la rue des Alchimistes à côté du château
        et de ses portes de nuages.

Avec les gestes d'un mime, Franz parle avidement
        de marcher jusqu'à minuit
et encore une fois à minuit pour arriver à un café de miracles.
        Jeune comique, il est

indifférent au climat, et quand l'ange de l'apocalypse
        a froid et cherche une tendresse
chaude, Kafka ouvre ses bras à l'ange, sonne la corne
        de bélier, et tout d'un coup,

notre gang est heureux et nous arrivons au jour
        du jugement où le gros Dieu,
parlant doucement en hébreu, nous accueille
        sous son beau parapluie cosmique.

Donc, souriant toujours comme Charlot disant
        son au revoir aigre triste,
Franz affamé demande à Dieu: Pourquoi faut-il que la mort
        nous asseye au Café Zéro?

Café Zero with Dr. Franz Kafka

In Prague I dine with Dr. Franz Kafka,
      the Houdini of the word,
at his home on the Street of the Alchemists by the castle
      and its cloud gates.

With mime gestures Franz is speaking eagerly
      about walking till midnight
and again till midnight to reach a café of miracles.
      A young comedian, he is

indifferent to climate, and when the Apocalypse angel
      shivers, hunting for warm
tenderness, Kafka opens his arms to the angel and blows
      the ram's horn. Suddenly

our gang is happy and we reach the day
      of judgment where fat God,
speaking softly in Hebrew, receives us under
      his gorgeous cosmic umbrella.

Then, ever smiling like Charley Chaplin saying
      his bitter-sad goodbye,
hungry Franz asks God: Why must death
      seat us at the Café Zero?

Café des Éditeurs

J'aime les cafés, ma maison vagabonde.
J'y vais pour parler, lire et rencontrer
des polyglottes et sophistes ou logiciens
qui peuvent soutenir le monde
sur une parole étourdissante, ou pour
me perdre dans l'isolement de la naissance.

J'adore the librairies et brasseries
et la rue de Mignon, nuit de Paris,
et les buchers et sténographes
qui dansent les fêtes du jour au violon
et l'accordéon. J'oublie le fléau
de l'esprit qui disparaît et devine
que je suis. La victoire est car tu es.

Je crache sur l'extinction. Elle est sans café
crème et futile de rouler. Je rêve.
Aucune réponse. Près du Luxembourg,
au Café des Éditeurs, je vois les livres
des disparus et je ris—ils sont vivants—
et insouciant je bois mon vide.

Café of the Editors

I love cafés, my vagabond house.
I go there to talk, read and find
polyglots or sophists or logicians
who can hold up the world
on one astonishing word or to lose
myself in the loneliness of birth.

I adore the bookstores and brasseries
and rue de Mignon a Paris night
where butchers and stenographers
dance on a saint's day to fiddle
and accordion. I forget the curse
of disappearing mind and guess
I am. A victory because you are.

I spit on extinction. She is foodless
and futile to outsmart. I dream.
No answer. Near Luxembourg Garden
at Café des Editeurs, I see the books
of the extinct and laugh—they are alive—
and cheerfully drink my emptiness.

Café du Néant

Dans la brume intérieure je cherche un moi
      visible ou un mot qui parle

d'une idée clef—mais où j'attends la lumière
      il n'est que l'abstraction

sans yeux du néant. Ce vide que je connais
      depuis la jeunesse et l'acte

d'explorer et d'échouer, et toujours je sors
      certain que je suis un creux

de nerfs. En effroi je m'accepte nulle part,
      la solitude dans le monde,

en sachant que c'est la condition normale
      mais personne ou presque

personne ne le reconnaît. Quand la brume
      et le fait de mon illusion

sont intolérables, j'écris, je me rappelle
      les mots d'un professeur

aveugle de philosophie qui m'a conseillé
      d'aller au cinéma,

ou je trouve refuge au café du néant,
      un beau café, misérable

de préférence, une cave à Prague qui pue
      le chou et la charcuterie,

Café of Nothingness

In the interior fog I hunt for a visible
      me or a speaking word

or a key idea—but where I wait for light
      there is an eyeless abstraction

of nothingness. The void I know since
      my youth and the habit

of exploring and failing. I always leave
      sure I am a hollow

of nerves. With dread I accept myself nowhere,
      a solitude in the world,

knowing this is the normal condition,
      but no one or almost

no one perceives it. When the fog
      and fact of my illusion

are intolerable, I write or I recall
      the words of a blind

professor of philosophy who advises me,
      "Go see a movie,"

or I find refuge in the Café of Nothingness,
      a pretty café, preferably

miserable, a cellar in Prague stinking
      of cabbage and sausage,

où tout le monde regarde l'étranger, y compris
    l'accordéoniste aveugle

qui me scrute fixement clouant ma solitude,
    ou je m'assois au café mémoire

dans le quartier d'étudiants à Paris où je vais
    pour oublier que je suis.

where everyone stares at the stranger, including
      the blind accordionist

who scrutinizes me, nailing my solitude,
      or sit at the memory café

in the student quarter in Paris where I go
      to forget that I am.

Café de la Nuit de Joie

Dans ce café de *La Jeunesse Éternelle*
(nom d'une fleur du Périgord),
le corbeau n'a qu'une aile énorme,
jaune et ne vole pas. Il boit à petits coups
du chocolat et dansent le Charleston.

Je suis comme mes amis du ciel:
regarde ce simple bouffon qui lit
dans une chaise de lune de Pluton,
et nous sommes tous obligés d'inventer
les paroles, car nos coeurs sont faibles,

et j'invente la joie qui m'élève
d'une tristesse profonde mais pas
philosophique. L'ignorance est l'extase
qui me permet ce qui n'est pas dans
ta tasse, en toi le patron de la France.

Patience. Que tu supportes ce gosse
quand l'orage rouge dit que c'est l'heure
du naufrage. L'âme n'existe guère
et moi et mon âme sommes des fables
de Guillaume ce soir de bonheur.

Café of a Night of Joy

In this café of *Eternal Youth*
(name of a flower from the Périgord),
the crow has only one enormous yellow
wing and doesn't fly. It sips
hot chocolate and dances the Charleston.

I am like my friends of the sky.
Just look at this simple buffoon reading
in a moon chair from Pluto,
and we all must invent words,
since ours hearts are weak,

and I devise a joy that raises me
from deepest but not philosophic
sorrow. Ignorance is the ecstasy
that allows me what is not in
your cup, in you the owner of France.

Patience. You put up with this kid
when the red storm says it is time
to shipwreck. The soul barely exists
and I and my soul are the fables
of Guillaume this evening of joy.

Café de Nuit

J'aime les longs dîners au Café de Nuit avec Vincent,

mon cousin de cœur. La foule d'Arles se promène

sur la place orange. Les maisons jaunes et des étoiles

énormes les observent. D'habitude, Vincent est déprimé.

Depuis mon enfance rien de nouveau. Comme il me dit,

il ne contrôle pas ses passions. Puis, Paul est parti

et il peint comme un fou, usant les tubes de pigment

comme des doigts d'amants pour embrasser la nature

et la nature brûle. Il me dit, «Guillaume, Que faire?»

«Idiot, tu as un lit, une chaise de bois et la passion?

Que veux-tu de plus?» «Du temps,» il me dit. La nuit est paon

comme ses couleurs. Après le dîner nous marchons

un peu et quand nous sommes chez lui, il m'offre

un calvados et placidement écrit un poème.

Night Café

I like the long suppers in the Night Café with Vincent,
my cousin of the heart. The mob at Arles strolls about
in the orange square. The yellow houses and enormous
stars observe him. Usually, Vincent is depressed.

Since my childhood that's nothing new. As he says,
he can't control his passions. Then, Paul leaves him
and he paints like a madman, using tubes of pigment
like the fingers of lovers to embrace nature

and nature burns. He says, "Guillaume, what can I do?"
"Idiot, you have a bed, a wooden chair and passion.
What else do you want?" "Time," he tells me.

The night is peacock like his colors. After the supper
we walk around a while and when we're at his place,
he offers me a calvados and peacefully writes a poem.

Café de l'Aube à Paris

Je dors et déjà vis demain. Lundi sera.
Mais non, c'est un beau dimanche matin négligent
et je danse avec Dieu, une belle femme

qui me dit bouche à bouche dans mon âme
les secrets banals de ma confusion, et pourquoi
je ne peux pas dormir, pourquoi obligé je me lève

du sommeil pour te parler dans le noir,
des heures avant le café de l'aube qui me sauve
sans doute. Je me trompe. J'embrasse la bouche

de Dieu. Elle est douce et ne me méprise pas
que je meure sans espoir. Elle m'assure
que sa présence n'est pas nécessaire, et je l'aime

dévasté par son dur éloignement. J'ai froid.
L'hiver sans remords gît sur mes genoux.
J'embrasse un fantôme. Chaude elle sourit.

Dawn Café in Paris

I sleep and already live tomorrow. Must be
Monday. No, a beautiful negligent Sunday morning
and I dance with God, a beautiful woman

who tells me mouth to mouth in my soul
the banal secrets of my confusion,
and why I can't sleep, why forced to I get up

from sleep to speak to you in the black
in hours before the café of dawn who saves me
surely. I'm wrong. I kiss the mouth

of God. She is soft and doesn't blame me
that I die without hope. She assures me
that her presence isn't necessary, and I love her

devastated by her remoteness.
I'm cold. Pitiless winter lies on my knees.
I kiss a phantom. Warm, she is smiling.

Note on Author

Born in Lewiston, Maine, Willis Barnstone was educated at Bowdoin, Columbia, Yale and the Sorbonne. He taught in Greece at the end of the civil war (1949-51), was in Buenos Aires during the Dirty War, and in China during the Cultural Revolution. A Guggenheim fellow, he has been the recipient of the NEA, NEH, the Emily Dickinson award from the Poetry Society of America, the W. H. Auden Award of the New York State Council on the Arts, and four Book-of-the-Month selections. His work has appeared in *American Poetry Review, Poetry, Harper's Magazine, New York Review of Books, The Nation, The New Republic, The Paris Review, The New Yorker*, and the *Times Literary Supplement*.

Other Books by Willis Barnstone

Poetry
Poems of Exchange
From This White Island
Antijournal
A Day in the Country
New Faces of China
China Poems
Overheard
A Snow Salmon Reached the Andes Lake
Ten Gospels and a Nightingale
The Alphabet of Night
Five A.M. in Beijing
Funny Ways of Staying Alive
The Secret Reader: 501 Sonnets
Algebra of Night: New & Selected Poems 1948-1998
Life Watch
Stickball on 88th Street

Translations
Eighty Poems of Antonio Machado (Introduction by John Dos Passos;
    Reminiscence by Juan Ramón Jiménez)
The Other Alexander: Greek Novel by Margarita Liberaki
    (with Helle Barnstone)
Greek Lyric Poetry
Physiologus Theobaldli Episcopi (*Bishop Theobald's Bestiary*)
Sappho: Poems in the Original Greek with a Translation
The Poems of Saint John of the Cross
The Song of Songs
The Poems of Mao Tse-Tung
My Voice Because of You: Pedro Salinas. Preface by Jorge Guillén
The Unknown Light: Poems of Fray Luis de León
A Bird of Paper: Poems of Vicente Aleixandre (Preface by Vicente Aleixandre;
    with David Garrison)

Laughing Lost in the Mountains: Poems of Wang Wei
    (with Tony Barnstone and Xu Haixin)
Six Masters of the Spanish Sonnet: Quevedo, Sor Juana Inés de la Cruz,
Machado, Lorca, Borges, Miguel Hernández
To Touch the Sky: Poems of Mystical, Spiritual and Metaphysical Light
Sonnets to Orpheus by Rainer Maria Rilke
Border of a Dream: Selected Poems of Antonio Machado
Sweetbitter Love: Poems by Sappho
Ancient Greek Lyrics
Love Poems of Pedro Salinas and Katherine Letter Poems

Memoir

With Borges on an Ordinary Evening in Buenos Aires
Sunday Morning in Fascist Spain: A European Memoir, 1948-1953
We Jews and Blacks: Memoir with Poems (with Yusef Komunyakaa)

Literary Criticism

The Poetics of Ecstasy: From Sappho to Borges
The Poetics of Translation: History, Theory, Practice
The ABC of Translation

Biblical

The Other Bible: Intertestamental Scripture
Apocalypse (Book of Revelation)
The New Covenant : Four Gospels and Apocalypse
The Gnostic Bible (with Marvin Meyer)
Masterpieces of Gnostic Wisdom (with Marvin Meyer)
The Restored New Testament, Including the Gnostic Gospels of Thomas,
Mary, and Judas

Anthologies / Editions

Modern European Poetry
Spanish Poetry from Its Beginnings through the Nineteenth Century
Eighteen Texts: Writings by Contemporary Greek Authors
Concrete Poetry: A World View (with Mary Ellen Solt)

A Book of Women Poets from Antiquity to Now
    (with Aliki Barnstone)
Borges at Eighty: Conversations
The Literatures of Asia, Africa, and Latin America
    (with Tony Barnstone)
Literatures of the Middle East (with Tony Barnstone)
Literatures of Latin America